THE
CONTRACTOR

THE
CONTRACTOR

HOW I LANDED IN
A PAKISTANI PRISON
and IGNITED A
DIPLOMATIC CRISIS

RAYMOND DAVIS

WITH STORMS REBACK

BenBella Books, Inc.
Dallas, TX

BenBella Books, Inc.
10440 N. Central Expressway, Suite 800
Dallas, TX 75231
www.benbellabooks.com
Send feedback to feedback@benbellabooks.com

Printed in the United States of America
10 9 8 7 6 5 4 3 2 1

Library of Congress Cataloging in Publication Control Number: 2016015154
ISBN 978-1-941631-84-3 (hardcover)

Editing by Leah Wilson and Vy Tran
Copyediting by James Fraleigh
Proofreading by Lisa Story, Greg Teague, and Rachel Phares
Text design by Publishers' Design and Production Services, Inc.
Text composition by PerfecType, Nashville, TN
Cover design by Pete Garceau
Jacket design by Sarah Avinger
Cover photo © ILYAS J.DEAN/PAK IMAGES/Newscom
Printed by Lake Book Manufacturing

Distributed by Perseus Distribution
www.perseusdistribution.com

To place orders through Perseus Distribution:
Tel: (800) 343-4499
Fax: (800) 351-5073
E-mail: orderentry@perseusbooks.com

Special discounts for bulk sales (minimum of 25 copies) are available. Please contact Aida Herrera at aida@benbellabooks.com.

For my son. I hope you will grow up in
a safer world than the one I've known, thanks,
in some measure, to the work I did overseas.

Author's Note

A LOT HAS BEEN WRITTEN about the time I spent in a Pakistani jail in 2011—much of it, unfortunately, false. I'm hoping to set the record straight. If I withhold anything, it's only to ensure that I don't divulge any information that could compromise our national security or put any American service personnel or contractors in harm's way. To that end, some names have been changed. This book represents my views and not those of the State Department or any one of the private military-contracting companies that have employed me. With only a few notable exceptions, the events described are based entirely on my memory. Because of the rigors of captivity and the absence of a watch or clock much of the time I was held, the timing of some events may be slightly off. A similar caveat applies to the dialogue. While I've done my best to recall the most important conversations I had during that time, the phrasing is almost certainly inexact.

1.

MOZANG CHOWK, LAHORE, PAKISTAN
(January 27, 2011—Day 1)

Funny, isn't it, how a bunch of very small and subtle decisions, when added together, can end up having such enormous consequences? I hadn't been awake more than an hour when I was presented with one such choice.

"There's only one SUV left outside," our team leader, a former Navy SEAL, informed me. "You need it? Or can I take it into the office?"

Our office was the US Consulate General in Lahore, Pakistan. As private military contractors, our job was to protect Americans working overseas, particularly those living in hostile environments. It might not have been the most glamorous occupation—some people called us glorified security guards, while others labeled us knuckle-draggers—but it was an essential one. Without us, many more Americans would have died while working abroad. It's as simple as that.

Thanks to the extremely rough roads that are so commonplace in South Asia, our vehicle of choice was an SUV. Let me share a quick story to give you an idea of just how tough and reliable they are. While working in Afghanistan, I once took a large SUV out on a long-range mission. The vehicle's frame broke, and we had to tow it back in with—yep, that's right—a smaller SUV. That the SUVs at our disposal were armored with steel only made them that much more desirable.

But I've always been a team player. "No problem. I'll use the white sedan today."

If you believe in chaos theory, which credits small changes in initial conditions with creating large (and often divergent) fluctuations in certain systems, my decision to drive a soft-skinned rental car around the streets of Lahore instead of an armored SUV was like the veritable butterfly flapping its wings halfway around the world. It kicked off a chain of events that would later be used as a case study at the John F. Kennedy School of Government at Harvard University to show how the accumulation of a number of small, seemingly innocuous missteps can quickly lead to a crisis. The incident that took place in Lahore, and that will forever be linked with my name, was a textbook case. A clerical error here, a diplomatic snub there, and suddenly you've got a major diplomatic crisis on your hands.

And it all started with me, a lowly contractor, typically a bit player in the wartime theater, volunteering to use a vehicle that was no match for the many challenges it was about to face.

If only I'd gotten up a little earlier that morning, maybe things would have turned out differently.

I'D FLOWN INTO ISLAMABAD, Pakistan's preplanned capital city, the week before, then down to Lahore the following day. This was my ninth trip to Pakistan in the last two years, half of which I'd spent in Peshawar, a frontier town near the border shared with Afghanistan. The other half I'd spent in Lahore, the capital of Punjab Province and the country's second-largest city. Home to nearly 10 million people as well as numerous universities, markets, archaeological sites, historic monuments, mosques, restaurants, and stadiums, Lahore was a bustling and vibrant city with a rich history and culture. It was also home to a fair number of terrorists, putting it on the front lines of the War on Terror.

Despite the exotic locale, my job was generally mundane, and that was just the way I liked it. In that way, my teammates and I were not unlike sports referees: If no one ever noticed us, that meant we were doing a great job. It was only on those rare occasions when something went wrong that we were forced to make our presence known.

As security contractors, one of our main responsibilities was protecting people from themselves. Don't get me wrong—most of the people I was charged with protecting were highly intelligent and very good at their jobs, but they simply weren't trained to recognize the possible dangers that could arise if they were to wander into the wrong place at the wrong time. They excelled in environments that were completely foreign to me—office buildings in Washington, DC, for example—but let them loose in a country where anti-American sentiment is strong and terrorist groups are prevalent and you have a potential disaster on your hands. I was there to make sure they didn't make any foolish choices, that they stayed safe and came home in one piece.

This task was made much harder when the people I was supposed to protect failed to heed my warnings. I was once put in charge of a group of US Agency for International Development (USAID) officials who were looking to build new houses and roads in a few small villages in rural Afghanistan. Before we set out, I warned everyone in the group that the country was heavily mined, and I implored them to be careful. I told them, "You can't wander off. Stay next to us and do exactly what we do." But, of course, one of them just had to take a picture of something, and the next thing I knew she was standing in the middle of an active minefield.

"Stop!" I yelled. "Do not take another step."

"Huh? Why?"

"Did you not see the red rock?" I pointed at the painted rock, which, to those who knew better and were paying attention, indicated the edge of the minefield.

Unable to think of a better plan, I had to walk into the minefield and guide the USAID official out of it, carefully retracing her steps. One wrong move and my wife would have gotten that awful knock on the door. But I didn't have a choice in the matter. Tiptoeing my way through a field full of improvised explosive devices (IEDs) was just part of the job. As a contractor, all you can do in a situation like this is concentrate on whatever needs to be done to resolve the problem and not get caught up worrying about the possible repercussions of someone else's bad decision. Getting killed is always a possibility, which ensures that you stay sharp from moment to moment but over the years creates a dull weariness in you.

I'd be lying if I said all the close calls I'd faced in my career didn't affect me. I was once asked to drive the lead car—we called it the "jammer"—for Dick Cheney's advance team while he was visiting Afghanistan during the war. My job was to break traffic, moving cars out of the way if necessary, to ensure that the vice president's convoy could get through. On our way from President Hamid Karzai's palace to the US Embassy in Kabul, a car appeared on the far left side of the highway and started making its way toward us. I asked my teammate who was riding shotgun to get on the radio and tell the other vehicles in the convoy to shift right, and then I downshifted and started driving straight at the oncoming car. My job was to protect the vice president's motorcade, which was close on our heels, at all costs, so if the car coming at us was carrying a vehicle-borne improvised explosive device (VBIED), I needed to make sure it detonated as far away from him as possible. If that meant I was going to be injured or even killed in the process, well, that was also part of the job. I actually tried to hit the oncoming car, but at the last second it veered away. That could have easily been *the day*, but I guess luck was on my side.

Coming to terms with the massive amount of randomness that exists in the universe was one of the hardest parts of the job. Step here and you're drinking beer with your buddies that night; step there and you're going home in a body bag. A contractor I worked with during multiple deployments in Afghanistan and Pakistan once illustrated the outsized role luck plays in a war zone or similarly hostile environment with a metaphor that's always stuck with me. The way he saw it, everyone is born with two theoretical jars, a Skill Jar and a Luck Jar. Every time you do something dangerous, one of the marbles from your Luck Jar moves into your Skill Jar, because while doing that activity you honed an ability that might save your life down the road.

At first, your Skill Jar is empty because you don't have any experience, but as you get more proficient at certain tasks, that jar starts to fill with marbles. This explains how so many of the grizzled war veterans who have extended their careers working as contractors—we called them Old Warriors—have managed to survive so long. After filling their Skill Jars, they tend to make better decisions and fewer life-threatening mistakes than they did before.

But where do all the marbles in your Skill Jar come from? From your Luck Jar. And here's the unfair part (of this metaphor and life in general): Everyone's Luck Jar doesn't start off with the same amount of marbles. Some of us may have very few to start, while others may have a lot. And when all the marbles in your Luck Jar are gone, that's it. You're done. No amount of skill can save you then. So every time you do something dangerous and survive, you need to remember that you now have one less marble in your Luck Jar, and if you continue to do the same life-threatening activity, year after year, like I did working in hostile environments overseas half my life, one day you're going to run out of marbles.

That you don't know exactly how many marbles you've got left at any given time creates a never-ending, existential quandary: Either you constantly worry about it or you don't worry about it at all. I chose the latter route, banishing the thought from my head as much as I could and devoting my energy to trying to get a little better at my job every single day.

AS I GOT BEHIND THE WHEEL of the white sedan and pulled out of the compound in Lahore's Scotch Corner neighborhood where my team was staying, the only thing I was thinking about was the task ahead of me. The purpose of this outing was to survey the route I'd be taking someone on three days later. I needed to pay close attention to any danger spots or anything that appeared out of the ordinary along the way. In a country like Pakistan, which remains one of the world's most fertile terrorist breeding grounds, you always have to be on the alert. Since the start of the War on Terror, there had been more than a dozen attacks in Pakistan against US diplomatic missions and businesses frequented by Americans, and the number of Pakistani civilians killed in terrorist-related violence in 2010 wasn't all that far behind the number of Afghan civilians killed that same year, even though Afghanistan was at war and Pakistan wasn't—at least not officially.

Despite how big Lahore was, it rarely felt overtly dangerous—unlike, say, Karachi, Pakistan's largest city, where terrorist attacks were quite common. And yet terrorist violence still occurred there from time to time. Lahore wasn't Baghdad, but it wasn't Kansas City, either. Anytime I traveled beyond the high walls that surrounded the house where my teammates and I lived, I grew more cautious. But vigilance does not retard humor. At one point during that morning's drive, I couldn't stop myself from laughing, just as I always did, when Katy Perry's "I Kissed a Girl" came on the radio. In the Pakistani version of the song, "girl" has been dubbed out of the chorus and replaced with "person," and—as if that wasn't awkward enough—it's done with a man's voice. Hearing this never failed to crack me up.

Katy Perry provided only a momentary distraction. As I drove down Mall Road, a wide street lined with beautiful old buildings built during the era when Pakistan was part of India and India was part of the British Empire, I was constantly scanning the area for any sort of suspicious activity. A bulge in a young man's waistline could mean he was carrying a gun. A vehicle heavily weighted down in the back could indicate it was carrying a VBIED. A woman wearing bulky clothes on a hot day might suggest she was wearing a suicide vest. I'd spent the last five days doing much the same thing, driving around the city, relearning its streets, taking the temperature of the environment, getting a feel for what was going on.

Whenever I drove in Lahore, I also had to be on the lookout for roadblocks and hastily improvised checkpoints. The relationship between Pakistan and the United States had become increasingly frayed in recent years, and one of the most obvious signs of this discord was how difficult it had become for Americans, particularly those attached to the embassy or one of the consulates, to move around the country. Vehicles with diplomatic license plates seemed to get pulled over more frequently and, after being stopped, harassed to a greater degree than the other cars on the road. After the police succeeded in stopping one of our vehicles, they would often try to get inside it, but we always refused to let them. We'd heard the horror stories about contractors in Iraq getting ambushed by militants wearing fake police uniforms, and we weren't about to fall for the same deadly trick. The police usually took our refusal as an affront and would often detain us, right there on the side of the road, for hours and hours, forcing the regional security officer—the RSO is the senior law enforcement officer at every US embassy and consulate—to come rescue us.

The Pakistani police even arrested an old lady whose job was to monitor a radio during the night shift at the consulate in Lahore. She looked like someone's grandmother, but they tried to paint her as a spy, claiming she was carrying "spy gadgetry" and an AK-47. The spy gadgetry turned out to be a digital camera, the AK-47 a complete fabrication. When the police couldn't produce any evidence that substantiated their claim, the Lahore High Court dismissed the case and the old woman was released.

As I drove around the city, I also paid close attention to traffic patterns, taking note of areas where I could get bogged down. On the day I volunteered to use the white sedan, traffic was flowing fairly smoothly until the busy thoroughfare I was on, Jail Road, which had three lanes going in each direction and a grassy median in between, approached an even busier street, Ferozepur Road. In Pakistan, this sort of major intersection is called a *chowk*, and this particular one, Mozang Chowk, surrounded as it was by a bus station and multiple banks and restaurants, was very busy and quite well known.

The closer I got to the intersection, the slower I was forced to go, until I finally came to a complete stop. Besides the two main roads, several smaller roads also fed into the intersection, further snarling traffic. I could see a traffic cop up ahead, doing his best to untangle the mess. In their distinctive blue uniforms, traffic cops were a common sight in Pakistan. Their main responsibilities were directing traffic and issuing tickets for moving violations—they didn't even carry guns—but from my experience all they ever did was make any problem they encountered worse.

When I came to a stop, I was in the middle lane of the three-lane road, about ten cars away from the intersection. The lanes to my right and left were both filled with cars, and the space in between the cars was filled with motorcycles, bicycles, rickshaws, and "tuk-tuks," which are mopeds that have enclosed cabs and three wheels. There were so many motorcycles around my car it felt like I was at the start of a motocross rally—but a uniquely Pakistani one. It wasn't unheard of there to see as many as seven people on a single motorcycle. I've also seen a Pakistani motorcyclist carrying an entire car windshield down the road and, more disturbingly, one holding an unrestrained baby. The only law there concerning motorcycle safety was that the driver had to wear a helmet. Beyond that, it was a free-for-all.

I sat at that intersection for about two minutes, scanning the area the entire time, a habit as ingrained in me as breathing, particularly when I'm boxed in by vehicles or caught in a crowd of people. I looked to my right, I looked to my left, and, using the rearview mirror, I checked directly behind me at my six o'clock position, or "six" for short. Satisfied that nothing out of the ordinary was going on, I returned my attention to the road straight ahead of me, and as I did I noticed a black motorcycle pull directly in front of me. On it were two men. The driver, who I would later learn was named Faizan Haider, was wearing a helmet and facing forward with both hands on the handlebars. The other man, Muhammad Faheem, was sitting directly behind Haider on the back of the bike, but his upper body was turned almost all the way around so that he was nearly facing me. I could see his hips. I could see his stomach. I could see his chest. And I could see his hand as it pulled a pistol from his waistband.

Guns are fairly common in Pakistan and, as most gun owners will attest, aren't in and of themselves dangerous. But when someone draws a gun in the middle of a crowded intersection, the equation changes. That person immediately becomes a threat.

When faced with a life-threatening situation, most people get overwhelmed and their bodies automatically shut down some of their senses, which increases their vulnerability. They lose their fine motor skills, rendering them unable to perform even the simplest tasks with their hands. They get tunnel vision as their eyes block out everything in the periphery in order to focus solely on the threat. And they get auditory exclusion, the aural version of tunnel vision, as their minds filter out every noise but the ones they consider most important. These reactions are all part of the normal fight-or-flight response humans have when subjected to extreme stress.

Fortunately, I'd been trained by some of the finest instructors in the world how to respond to just this sort of threat. By taking a deep breath, I was able to control my stress level to the point where I could still see everything in front of me as well as in my periphery. Most people would have focused exclusively on the gun, but for me it felt like I was staring at a 65-inch, widescreen, high-definition television, and I could take in every single inch of it at the same time. Everything in front of me was crystal clear. I could see every speck of dirt on my windshield. I could see all the cars up ahead of me. I could see the rickshaws and tuk-tuks to the left and right of me. I could see the brake lights of the motorcycle directly in front of my car. And I could clearly see the two men on the bike. They appeared to be Pakistani, but I couldn't identify much about them beyond that. They weren't wearing uniforms that would indicate they were part of the police or military. They were, as far as I could tell, just a couple of guys.

That is, just a couple of guys with a gun. The gun ultimately demanded my full attention. Time seemed to slow to a crawl as I watched the guy on the back of the motorcycle rack it and start to take aim. When I first noticed him pull the gun from his waistband, it was pointing down, but now its muzzle slowly began to rise, first pointed at the grille of my car, then at the hood, before inching its way upward until it was level with, and pointed directly at, me.

2.

BIG STONE GAP, VIRGINIA
(October 1979)

L IFE WAS NEVER EASY where I grew up. Big Stone Gap, Virginia, is a blink-and-you-miss-it town tucked into the mountains in the most isolated part of the state. It's actually farther west than any point in *West* Virginia and is much closer to the capitals of Kentucky, Tennessee, and North Carolina, in both distance and philosophy, than it is to its own state's capital of Richmond.

This was coal country, and my dad worked in the mines right up until the day a 700-pound rock fell on top of him, breaking his back in three places. I was only five years old at the time, but the impact of my dad's injury was clear to me. While he recovered, my mom had to work three jobs just to make ends meet. Money was always tight. My brother and sister and I never actually starved. Most Americans equate being hungry with starving, but these two conditions aren't even remotely close. Starving isn't forgetting to eat lunch because you were too busy at work. Starving is going two weeks without food. My family never starved. But we often went hungry. More than a few times we had to make a batch of cornbread and mashed potatoes last the whole week.

I never thought all that much about it because so few people living in Wise County were very well-off. A large percentage of them were living so far below the poverty line that that elusive measure might as well have been marking the edge of outer space. The good news? When everyone around you is just as poor as you are, it doesn't feel like poverty anymore but something closer to normal. It was only after I left that I realized just how poor my family really was.

Growing up, I was always one of the bigger kids in my grade. As a seventh grader, I made the eighth-grade football team, even though I really didn't know what I was doing. All I knew how to do was get in front of a guy and block him when we were on offense and tackle whoever had the ball when we were on defense. But I was big and strong and fast, and that made up for a lot.

My dad was always very supportive of my athletic career. He enjoyed watching me play so much he'd even come to my practices and sit in the bleachers. He got so into it during this one scrimmage that he actually started yelling at my coach to put me in. The coach responded with a chuckle and a why-not sort of gesture, then tried me out at nose guard. I played well enough that the coach started giving me a lot more playing time. I played offensive guard and defensive tackle throughout high school, and as a senior I got to block for a speedy freshman running back named Thomas Jones. The first time he ever touched the ball, he bounced from one sideline to the other, probably running more than sixty yards just to move the ball a few yards past the line of scrimmage. In the huddle, he was shaking he was so scared or amped up—it was hard to tell which—and we reminded him to run north and south, not east and west. He responded by rushing for a long touchdown on the very next play. He went on to run for 10,591 yards in the NFL, putting him in twenty-fifth place on the all-time list, but I'll always remember him as that kid who was wide-eyed with fright and adrenaline during our game against the J. J. Kelly Indians.

I also wrestled and ran track in high school, but, unfortunately, my dad didn't get to see me do any of that. He died of a heart attack when I was fourteen. Paying the bills hadn't been easy when he was with us, so you can imagine what it was like with him gone. We had to go on food stamps and collect Supplemental Security Income. Dealing with that kind of adversity at such a young age either breaks you or makes you stronger, and I wasn't about to let it break me. I refused to adopt a woe-is-me attitude. Instead, I did whatever I could to help my family put food on the table. In the fall, I chopped wood. In the winter, I shoveled snow. The rest of the year, I laid brick and block for $10 an hour. That was a small fortune for a fifteen-year-old. I'd take $25, sometimes $50, out of each paycheck for myself and give the rest to my mom.

I got so good at bricklaying that I actually won district and state championships in that pursuit and went on to finish eighteenth in the nationals. As soon as I graduated from high school, I got bombarded with job offers from all over the country, from New York all the way to California, promising me a decent wage laying brick. But just as I knew I didn't want to work in the mines, I knew I didn't want to lay brick the rest of my life. More than anything, I wanted to get out of Big Stone Gap and see the world, which was how I ended up at the local Armed Forces recruiting office. I tried to join the Marines, but their recruiter kept blowing me off. He was more interested in tall, skinny kids, and I, built like a tree stump, was nearly the opposite. Taking the hint, I approached the army recruiter.

"What kind of jobs do you have available?" I asked him.

"Oh, we've got all kinds. But first let's get you a test and see where you're at."

I took the test and gave it back to him. He graded it and said, "Nice work. You scored high enough to be a 68 Whiskey."

"What the heck's that?"

"A medic."

"Like a doctor?"

"Yeah."

"I don't want to do that. I want to be outside. Don't you have anything where I can be outside?"

The army recruiter grinned at me like a used car salesman. "Sounds like you want be in the infantry."

"Yeah, the infantry. That's what I want to do."

"Let me see," he said, scrolling down his computer screen. "We just might have an open spot there."

Of course they had an open spot in the infantry. The army *always* has an open spot in the infantry. Later on, I also learned that 68 Whiskeys were actually *field* medics, which meant they worked outside in support of the infantry. That was how little I knew at the time. But I didn't let my ignorance dampen my enthusiasm. I was too excited about the path leading out of Big Stone Gap I'd forged for myself and the new identity I'd assumed. I was now an 11 Mike, an infantryman, in the US Army.

A few days later, I flew down to Fort Benning in Georgia. It was the first time I'd ever flown in a plane and the farthest I'd ever been away from home.

I was eighteen years old.

I THOUGHT I'D SERVE four years in the army, then get out, maybe go to college, try out for the football team, and see what civilian life was all about. Special Forces (SF) derailed that plan.

I was stationed at Fort Lewis, just south of Tacoma, Washington, and my four-year commitment to the army was almost up when I had the opportunity to spend an entire day on the shooting range with a bunch of SF guys. One of the primary missions of SF is to train soldiers, particularly foreign ones, so the reputation its members have earned for being first-rate instructors is deserved. Out on the range those guys showed us how to use weapons we might not have been familiar with, and, making the day that much more enjoyable, they weren't frugal with their ammunition. In fact, it seemed like they had so much ammo at their disposal they couldn't possibly shoot it all by themselves. We shot rifles at targets as far as 600 yards out and detonated a variety of explosives. That day was—I can't help myself—a blast, and at the end of it, the SF guys told us they were going to be doing it again the very next day. When we got back to our barracks, we grumbled aloud about what a horrible time we'd had before quietly volunteering to return to the range in the morning.

Somehow we got away with our little ruse, and we had just as much fun the second day as we'd had the first. As entertaining as it was, I got a lot more out of the experience than the pleasure of blowing stuff up. I came away impressed not only by the professionalism and the amount of knowledge the SF guys possessed but also by their easygoing attitudes. For guys who took their jobs so seriously and did them so well, they were incredibly laid back and pleasant to be around. After spending two days on the range with them, it was clear to me that their unit was in an entirely different league than what I was used to, that they had the best job in the entire United States Armed Forces, and that I wanted nothing more in the world than to be one of them.

Of course, getting into an elite outfit like SF isn't easy. For the next several months, all I did was train. Well, all I did *in addition to my regular duties as team leader*. Every morning, I got up at 4:30, did 100 pull-ups and 200 push-ups, and ran six miles, my pace dictated by the fact that I had to make it back to formation by 6:30. Then for the next two-plus hours I led my men through an equally grueling physical training session, which I did right alongside them. And every evening after work, I "ruck marched"—that is, carried a heavy rucksack full of gear—at least ten miles. This was my daily routine, and it got me in the best shape of my life, which was exactly what I needed to be in to get into SF.

After surviving this grueling schedule, I decided to try my hand at the Special Forces Assessment and Selection (SFAS) process. During this extremely rigorous three-week course, designed to push your body to its limit and weed out the weak, the other candidates and I probably walked more than 500 miles each while carrying rucksacks as heavy as seventy pounds. We were required to perform physically demanding tasks such as negotiating a land navigation course, alone, at night, in the rain, over rough terrain, while being timed; carrying full water cans in each hand ten kilometers down a dirt road; working with a twelve-man team to lift and carry a three-wheeled Jeep with poles; and working with a smaller team to carry a 350-pound duffel bag full of sand on a litter we'd fashioned from poles and a poncho. Typically, more than half the candidates in each SFAS course quit before it was done. And a good percentage of those who did finish were declared "Non-Selects" and told they needed to do it all over again. Non-Selects were allowed two more chances, but most guys, if they didn't get in the first time, never came back. Thanks to all the hard work I'd put in, I passed the course the first time I tried, but, as great a feeling as that was, all it really meant was that I'd cleared the first of many hurdles that stood between me and the gold-and-teal insignia and green beret worn by members of SF.

Next came the extremely challenging SF Qualification Course, which takes more than a year to complete. It's so long and intense that it's broken up into phases. In one phase, we learned (or, in my case, relearned) infantry tactics. In another phase, we were trained how to do our MOS. In the army, you don't have a "job"; you have a Military Occupational Specialty (MOS). In SF, my MOS was 18 Bravo, or Weapons Sergeant. There was also a language phase where I studied French for four months, and, finally, the culmination phase, aka "Robin Sage," where we put it all together and worked as an SF team in a highly realistic simulation of war, parachuting into hostile territory, eating whatever we could scavenge, and doing our best to avoid the enemy.

Tucked into this yearlong military grad school was the Survival, Evasion, Resistance, and Escape (SERE) course. An under-the-radar program dating back to the Korean War, it was designed to teach American military personnel how to avoid getting captured and, if that failed, how to hold up under questioning and withstand torture. For three weeks, we lived off the land in the snake-ridden backcountry of North Carolina while attempting to elude an unnamed and oftentimes unseen enemy. That was the easy part. Once we were captured—it's never a question of *if* but *when*—we were put through the same sort of abuse we might expect to receive if seized by an enemy who refused to abide by the Geneva Conventions.

SERE training was even more demanding—physically, mentally, and emotionally—than SFAS, and while taking part in it, I sustained some damage to my right lung. The injury occurred in 1998, but its full impact didn't make itself known until the fall of 2001, when my lung suddenly stopped working. The army responded by putting me on its Temporary Disability Retirement List. This meant I couldn't return to my job until the injury had fully healed and I was deemed fit for duty. In the wake of 9/11, you can imagine how devastated I was. It felt like I'd trained my entire life for the big game, and after we'd finally made it to the Super Bowl, I was stuck on the sidelines.

I offered to be an instructor while my lung healed, but the army rejected the idea. Plan B involved moving to Lexington, Kentucky, with my girlfriend, Rebecca, a fellow member of the 82nd Airborne Division I'd met at Fort Bragg. She got out of the army just before I did, after getting injured while jumping out of a plane. There were 30 mph winds that day, and you're not supposed to jump when it's blowing that hard, but the instructors refused to cancel the jump because some political higher-ups were there to watch. That wind carried all ninety-eight pounds of her clear across the drop zone, and she landed on her head, hitting the ground so hard it knocked her out and severely injured her neck and jaw. When she recovered, she was ready to move on to the next phase of her life.

We moved to Lexington so I could attend Eastern Kentucky University, which offered a unique course—Assets Protection & Security—I was interested in studying. I tried to make the best of collegiate life, but I can't lie: I was miserable. When I joined SF, it was like Christmas morning every time I woke up. I couldn't wait to get to work to find out what I was going to be doing that day. I loved my job. Going from that sort of sustained joy to having to sit in a classroom all day and barely being able to walk because I couldn't breathe was really tough. I was starting to get a little depressed when I came across a magazine article about an eight-year-old who'd had both legs amputated but still managed to run a mile in eight minutes. That snapped me out of my funk and motivated me to rehab my lung. I started walking as much as I could. When I could do that without gasping for air, I started riding a mountain bike. And when I could do that without any difficulties, I began to run. By following this routine, I was able to increase my lung capacity from a low of 52 percent all the way up to 89 percent.

With my right lung almost fully healed, I tried to return to SF in 2003, but the doctor refused to sign off on it. The army wouldn't even let me return to the infantry. All it could offer me was a 71 Lima MOS, an Administrative Specialist position, shuffling papers inside an office building all day long.

I couldn't bring myself to do it. Not because I felt like I was too good for such work. I believe every job in the army serves an important function. And not because I was intimidated by all the paperwork, although, admittedly, that's not my strong suit. No, I turned down the job offer because I knew what the atmosphere inside the administrative office was like, and let's just say it was as un-army-like as it could possibly be. I have a vivid memory of visiting the administrative office when I was an E-6, a Staff Sergeant, and having an encounter with an E-4, a Specialist—a rank that's earned a reputation for attracting those who like to avoid responsibility—that left a bad taste in my mouth. The E-4 had the nerve to address me, a superior officer, as, "Big Sarge," before asking me, "What up?" Such informality shocked and infuriated me. When I served in the army, I always respected the rank of my superiors while expecting those beneath me to do the same. Coming from the infantry and SF, I knew that if I took that clerk job I would lose my mind trying to work with people who had so little respect for the army's rules, protocols, and procedures.

I ended up doing one of the hardest things I've ever had to do, much harder than doing 100 pull-ups and 200 push-ups every morning or jumping out of an airplane or subsisting on grubs and worms for days at a time.

"I'm not pushing papers at a desk for the next twenty years," I told Rebecca. "I quit."

3.

FORT BRAGG, NORTH CAROLINA
(September 1999)

W HEN I MET RAY IN 1999, *I really wasn't interested in being with anybody, especially somebody from the military. I'd just broken up with a guy who was in the army and he was kind of a jerk, so I didn't want anything to do with another military guy. My plan was to get out of the army and go back home to Arizona and only date men who worked nine to five. I maintained my resolve until the night I went out to celebrate my birthday. There was a really long line to get into this bar, and I picked out the cutest and most approachable guy I could find in line and asked him if I could cut in front of him. Even though I had a bunch of friends with me, he said yes, and as big as he was, no one standing in line behind him said a word about it.*

That guy was Ray.

He and I became really good friends after that. I liked him because he wasn't a typical army guy. He was masculine and macho, but he didn't go out of his way to act that way. He wasn't a knuckle-dragging meathead. He actually had a soft side. Soon after we met, I was supposed to be in a friend's wedding and I was trying to figure out which shade of purple nail polish to get, and he sat on the floor in Walmart with me and helped me pick out one that matched my dress. He'd get pedicures with me. We had a lot of fun together. We were always on the same sheet of music. He quickly became my best friend, my rock. Soon, everyone started pushing us to date. "You would make such a great couple," they said. Finally, after several months of this, I gave in.

I especially liked how calm and easygoing Ray was and how he never talked down to anyone. These traits, when combined, made him a really good teacher. One day, soon after we began dating, Ray tracked me down on one of the shooting ranges at Fort Bragg just to say hi. While he was out there, he ended up helping some Maintenance Control Officers (MCOs) with their shooting. MCOs are part of a logistics unit. They don't get to shoot very often, so they were having a really hard time. Watching Ray help those MCOs and seeing how patient he was made me realize just how much I admired him. I could tell he'd be a great husband and—who knows?—maybe a great father as well some day.

THE FIRST TIME *Ray brought me to Big Stone Gap, I was shocked and humbled to see how poor everyone there was. I grew up just outside of San Francisco, so visiting a slice of Appalachia was definitely a culture shock for me. We were also fairly poor growing up, but it was macaroni-and-cheese-and-Spam poor. Ray's family was in much worse shape than that. After his dad got hurt, they had to go on food stamps, and Ray once confided in me, "If the stamps ran out on Wednesday, we wouldn't have food until Friday."*

The way he ate when we first met, it was like he was scared someone was going to take his plate away from him. He would just inhale his food. "Did you even taste it?" I'd ask. He'd eat everything on his plate in five minutes. I'd have to tell him, "Don't worry. There's more food. You don't have to eat the plate." He just had that mentality that each meal might be his last so he should make the most of it. Even though logically he knew that wasn't the case, I think it was drilled somewhere deep in his psyche that he might not get any more food for a very long time, so he needed to eat as much as he could while it was available.

When you think about Loretta Lynn's story—you know, Coal Miner's Daughter*—Ray's upbringing was a lot like that.*

AFTER WE GOT OUT OF THE ARMY *and moved to Lexington, Kentucky, Ray tried to do the college thing, but quickly realized it wasn't for him. I made him finish. I nagged him until he graduated because for a lot of people from his part of the country, going to college isn't even an option. Plus, he didn't have to pay for any of it. I had to pay $40,000 to get my degree and ended up joining the army just to pay off my student loans, but the VA paid for every one of Ray's pencils, every eraser,* everything.

I told Ray, "You're going to take advantage of this opportunity for all the people who can't."

I loved going to college. I got two degrees—one in Speech Pathology and another in Elementary and Special Education—and I had a great time. But it definitely wasn't for Ray. He would have much rather been in the army. That was his passion. It really was. He ate, slept, and drank it. He'd rather be on a team than anything else. He'd rather be out there, not showering for days on end, growing a beard, serving his country. That was his thing. When that was taken away from him, he was lost. He tried to do the civilian thing—go to college, get a job—but after three years he'd had enough.

"I don't want to do this anymore," he told me. "It's just not for me. I'm done."

I could tell he was serious. If Ray says he's not going to do something, then he's not going do it. That's just the way he is. For instance, soon after I first met him, he stopped drinking alcohol for an entire year. He just woke up one day and decided he was going to take a break from drinking, and guess what? For the next twelve months, he didn't consume a single drop. Combine that sort of determination with all the training he'd had, and you have a very powerful combination. When Ray gets something in his head, there's no changing his mind. That's how strong-willed he can be. And stubborn. I call it "stupid stubborn."

Unable to return to the army, Ray applied for a job as a private military contractor in 2004 after a friend told him one of the big companies was hiring. Ray told me about it in the kitchen. He said, "If you don't want me to do it, I won't."

But, honestly, how could I say no?

"I'm only going to do it for a year," he said.

But I knew.

"I promise. Just one year, then I'll try something else."

What he was saying sounded good, but I knew he was going to end up doing it a lot longer. I knew it because I knew Ray. What I didn't know was how it would end.

But I had a feeling about that, too. When I signed off on him becoming a contractor, I had a good idea that our marriage was over before it had even officially begun, but I buried that feeling deep down inside me and hoped and prayed that I was wrong.

We got married in March of that year. Ray actually picked out my wedding dress. I was happy. I was excited. We were starting a new life together. And Ray seemed every bit as happy and excited as I was.

Then two months later, he flew to Afghanistan for his first contracting job, and, to be honest, he never really came back.

4.

KABUL, AFGHANISTAN

(June 2004)

W HEN PEOPLE HEAR "military contractor," they tend to think "mercenary" (or even "soldier of fortune" or "hired gun"), but that's a misperception. A mercenary simply fights for a paycheck, regardless of which country is cutting it. Every military contractor I've ever known has viewed the job as an extension of his military career and would only sign on with an American company working in the best interests of the United States. Everything I did during my career as a contractor, I did in an effort to protect my country from the threat of terrorism and, as I'd sworn to do as an enlisted man, to "support and defend the Constitution of the United States against all enemies, foreign and domestic."

The US military's use of private contractors is as old as the country itself, dating all the way back to the American Revolution, when George Washington hired civilians to drive wagon trains, build temporary housing, cook meals, and tend to wounded soldiers in support of his Continental Army. This sort of arrangement—employing civilians to assist a war effort—took on a more businesslike quality during the Vietnam War, when a consortium of private corporations, dubbed the "Vietnam Builders," was awarded a no-bid $380 million contract to build airports, bases, roads, and hospitals in South Vietnam.

One of the biggest Vietnam Builders was Brown & Root, a company that had started as a small Texas roadbuilding concern before being awarded a lucrative contract in 1937 to build the Marshall Ford Dam (later renamed Mansfield Dam) just outside of Austin, Texas. The process was expedited by a young congressman named Lyndon Baines Johnson.

When LBJ ended up in the White House two decades later, Brown & Root continued to win large contracts for federally financed construction projects, and some began to suggest that the firm's good fortune might somehow be connected to the many large contributions it had given to LBJ's political campaigns over the years.

One of Brown & Root's more vocal critics was Illinois representative Donald H. Rumsfeld, who in 1966 called for an investigation into the relationship between the company and President Johnson. "Why this huge contract has not been and is not now being adequately audited is beyond me," he said before Congress. "The potential for waste and profiteering under such a contract is substantial."

In a remarkable about-face thirty-five years later, Rumsfeld, while serving as secretary of defense under President George W. Bush, introduced a new policy at the Pentagon calling for a much greater use of contractors from the private sector in nearly every aspect of the military, *including combat*, as part of what the press labeled the "Rumsfeld Doctrine."

Rumsfeld's initiative worked in almost perfect harmony with a proposal set forth by President George H. W. Bush's secretary of defense, Dick Cheney. In 1992, Cheney hired Brown & Root to conduct a $3.9 million study examining how the US military could fully maximize the benefits of the army's Logistics Civil Augmentation Program (LOGCAP), which was created in 1985 to formalize the relationship between the army and the contractors it depended upon for logistical support. The classified report produced by Brown & Root fostered a sea change in the way government contracts were issued. In the future, the LOGCAP contract would be given to a single company, which would in turn hire subcontractors, and—in a move that should surprise no one—Brown & Root, now known as Kellogg Brown & Root, was awarded the very first one.

DynCorp International was awarded the second LOGCAP contract, and after making it through its laborious enrollment process (I had to submit a résumé; pass psychological, physical fitness, and shooting tests; and take a three-week training course that covered personal security detail work, first aid, and advanced driving skills), I was hired to work in Afghanistan in 2004 for $600 a day.

What was good for me and my family was also good for the American taxpayer, because using contractors was shown to make good economic sense. At a 2005 symposium in Washington, DC, Erik Prince, the CEO and founder of one of the biggest private military contracting companies, Blackwater USA, addressed this very issue. "There's consternation in the DOD [Department of Defense] about increasing the permanent size of the army," he said. "We want to add 30,000 people, and they talked about costs of anywhere from $3.6 to $4 billion to do that. Well, by my math, that comes out to about $135,000 per soldier . . . We could certainly do it cheaper."

By nearly all measures, increasing the contractor-to-soldier ratio was a more cost-effective way of fighting a war. According to a 2006 Congressional Research Service report, it cost nearly $400,000 to keep one US soldier in Iraq in 2005. Depending on which report you subscribe to, that figure jumped to somewhere between $600,000 and $1.3 million in the years that followed, as the United States continued to pursue its two-front war in Iraq and Afghanistan. Compared to those astronomical figures, $200,000 or less to employ a military-trained contractor for a year overseas was a bargain.

During my first tour of Afghanistan, I was part of a team whose primary responsibility was protecting Hamid Karzai during his campaign to become his country's first democratically elected president. A slightly built man with a graying beard, Karzai once served as the head of his family's Pashtun tribe, the Popalzai, before being named interim president of Afghanistan after the United States overthrew the Taliban regime in 2001. He also spoke fluent English (as well as four other languages) and had spent considerable time in the United States and Europe, making him an ideal candidate for the United States to back in the all-important 2004 election, despite his occasionally erratic behavior.

A shockingly large percentage of Afghanistan's leaders have been assassinated, and by allying himself with the United States in 2001 Karzai made himself an even bigger target. On September 5, 2002, after returning to his hometown of Kandahar for his younger brother's wedding, Karzai was leaving Governor Gul Agha Sherzai's compound when an assassin disguised as a member of the palace guard drew a pistol and fired a flurry of shots in Karzai's direction. None of the shots hit their intended target, although Sherzai and a US Special Operations officer were wounded in the exchange. The Navy SEALs who were on Karzai's security detail shot and killed the would-be assassin along with, unfortunately, the two Afghans who'd tackled the shooter.

At this stage of the war, SEALs were in extremely high demand, and when this particular team was assigned a different mission and pulled off Karzai's detail, the State Department replaced it with a group of private security contractors managed by the Diplomatic Security Service (DSS). To be on this detail, you had to have experience working with one of the Special Operations Forces, which meant, as a former Green Beret, I jumped to the top of the list. This was the first assignment of my post-SF career, and soon after signing the contract I flew to Kabul and joined my new team.

I wasn't in Afghanistan very long before I found myself in an extremely dicey situation. We were responsible for protecting Karzai while he met with Ismail Khan, a former leader of the *mujahedin*, the CIA-funded Islamic radicals who stood up to the Soviet army during its invasion of Afghanistan in the 1980s. As governor of the Herat Province, Khan ruled the region as if it were his own personal kingdom, pocketing the taxes he collected on goods imported from neighboring Iran and Turkmenistan instead of sending them to the central government in Kabul. Karzai was hoping to discuss the idea of Khan becoming his vice president, but their potential union was beset by problems from the very beginning. Khan insisted that their meeting take place at his compound in a remote valley in the mountains, and when we arrived and got out of our vehicles in the middle of his courtyard, we were greeted by AK-47s. Khan's men were standing on the roof of the building that surrounded us and had their weapons aimed directly at us. We were also armed, but Khan's men controlled the high ground, so they had the tactical advantage.

A DSS agent was the officer in charge that day, and he got very agitated and started shouting orders. Instead of defusing the tension, he added to it. At one point, he raised the M4 rifle he was carrying in an aggressive manner, prompting the men on the roof to start shouting and zeroing in on us. All that my teammates and I could do was formulate a plan. One of us would whisper, "I've got this guy, this guy, and this guy." The man next to him would respond by saying, "Okay, I'll take the five guys on the other side of the courtyard." And so on down the line, each of us choosing a sector of fire.

It was an extremely tense situation, a true Mexican standoff, and all I could do was keep my internal warrior on high alert while exhibiting, as best I could, my external diplomat. I tried to project a sense of calm, but the DSS agent wasn't helping, continuing to shout orders and wave his gun around. Taking charge of the situation, our team leader took the DSS agent's gun away from him, shoved him inside one of our vehicles, and told him to stay there, successfully de-escalating a potential catastrophe.

We'd gotten lucky. That situation easily could have spiraled into a shootout, with us at a severe disadvantage, but our team leader saw a way to defuse the tension and seized it. We were taught that if you have a chance to extricate yourself from a dangerous situation such as that one, you always have to take it. The last thing any of us wanted was to make the headlines or, worse, get sent home in a body bag. Much better to live to fight another day.

It's a lesson I never forgot.

5.

MOZANG CHOWK, LAHORE, PAKISTAN
(January 27, 2011—Day 1)

I F I COULD HAVE FOUND a way out of the difficult position I found myself in at Mozang Chowk on January 27, 2011, with the man on the back of the motorcycle pointing a gun at me from no more than ten feet away, I would have gladly taken it. If I could have stomped on the gas and driven off, I would have done it, but that option wasn't available to me. It was bumper-to-bumper traffic. I couldn't drive forward, and I couldn't drive backward. I couldn't go right, and I couldn't go left. I was stuck. Of course, if I'd been in one of our armored SUVs, I wouldn't have had to do *anything*. I could have just sat inside of it and laughed if I'd wanted to, knowing that any shots fired at me would have bounced harmlessly off the windshield's bullet-resistant glass. Worst-case scenario: I would have had to take the damaged vehicle into the consulate the next day to get it repaired. But because I was driving a thin-skinned vehicle, I was a sitting duck. At that point, all I could do was rely on my training. If my life was being threatened, I was trained to defend myself, so that was exactly what I did.

As soon as I saw the gun's muzzle moving in my direction, I unclicked my seatbelt and started to draw the gun I was carrying in a waistband holster beneath the front of my shirt. This holster location was a personal preference. Some people like to carry their weapon on their lower back. Others prefer to carry it on their hip or chest. I've always preferred the appendix carry position. And it was a good thing, too. If I'd been carrying my gun on my back, I would have had a hard time getting to it in time because my hand would have gotten blocked by the seat. As it was, to get to my gun I still had to pull up the button-down shirt I was wearing, as well as the T-shirt I had on underneath that. Doing this might have added a couple hundredths of a second to my draw time, but that was about it.

How do I know this? Because I'd been training for moments like this my entire life.

I GREW UP SHOOTING SHOTGUNS in the woods with my brother and his friends. When I joined the army and went to Fort Benning for basic training, my drill instructor tried to make this out to be a liability.

"Who here's from the country?" he asked.

Everyone pointed at me because of my molasses-thick accent and aw-shucks demeanor.

The instructor got in my face. "I guarantee you're not going to pass this course because you grew up shooting your daddy's shotgun and you're not going to listen to a single word I say."

He was wrong about me. I've always been an avid learner. I don't care if I already know how to do something. If someone who knows more than I do wants to help me get better at a task, I'm always eager to learn more. During basic training I listened to every word that instructor had to say and absorbed all the knowledge presented to me, and I went on to receive the army's highest Marksmanship Qualification Badge. According to the army, when it came to shooting a gun, I was an expert.

I learned even more after I joined SF and became a weapons specialist, mostly by listening to the guys on my team who entered, and often won, shooting competitions like those put on by the International Defensive Pistol Association. Not only were these guys nationally ranked marksmen, they were also world-class instructors. They would show me little techniques that would dramatically improve my draw time and accuracy, and I soaked up every bit of information they threw my way.

One of the instructors gave me a tip that I still rely on today. "You know the difference between a professional shooter and a person who's just starting out?" he asked me.

I shook my head.

"A person just starting out works on the fundamentals and tries to do them perfectly. A professional shooter does the fundamentals perfectly, only he does them at a much faster rate. Once you've mastered the fundamentals, at that point you're just trying to get faster."

That advice always stuck with me. After hearing it, if I ever found my shooting skills eroding, I would simply take a step back and work on my fundamentals at a slower speed. Then, once I'd regained my accuracy and confidence, I'd work on getting faster.

While working as a contractor, I also performed a dry-fire drill—drawing an unloaded gun and firing it—every single night. I did this over and over again for twenty minutes. Thanks to all this practice, I got very fast at drawing my gun. Using a hip holster, I could draw and shoot, on average, in just under a second. Sometimes I was even able to get off two rounds in under a second. I was a little slower drawing from the appendix carry position, but not by much. My fastest time—including lifting my shirt, drawing my gun, aiming it, and firing—was .95 of a second, while my average was 1.1 seconds. That's about as long as it takes a hummingbird to flap its wings fifty times or a plane to travel 800 feet. Pretty darn fast, all things considered.

THE TWO MEN ON THE MOTORCYCLE that pulled in front of me at the intersection of Jail and Ferozepur Roads couldn't have known how fast I was at drawing my weapon. If they had, they probably would have chosen to ambush someone else. As soon as my gun cleared the steering wheel and was aimed at my intended target, I started pressing rounds out of the chamber, squeezing them off as I would with a fully automatic weapon. When I started shooting, I wasn't at full extended gun, with my arms straight out in front of me. My arms were actually bent. There are a lot of different terms for it, but I call this "mid-gun shooting."

In the United States, windshields are made with laminated safety glass that, if shattered, breaks into thousands of small round pieces, but most windshields in Pakistan aren't manufactured this way. The bullets I was using actually burned their way straight through the sedan's windshield. A tight pattern of round holes where my bullets had passed through appeared in the glass, while the windshield itself remained intact.

The gun I used, a brand-new Glock 17, had been issued to me upon my arrival in Lahore. Everything else I'd been given for the job—the GPS, camera, phone, and Motorola two-way radio—had been used by the contractor I'd replaced, just as I would pass these items along to the contractor who would replace me once my time in country was up. That's how it was in Pakistan. It was such a volatile country that there was always a need for more security contractors, and we came and went through a revolving door. I'd never even fired the gun before. One of my teammates joked about it after he, too, was issued a brand-new gun. He said, "Man, we've never even fired these guns. How do we know they shoot?"

Well, the one I was given shot just fine. Perfectly, in fact. I'd left the house that morning with seventeen rounds in the magazine and one in the chamber, and while defending myself at Mozang Chowk, I squeezed off ten as I aimed for the two men on the motorcycle.

And in a matter of two or three seconds, the entire engagement, from the moment I saw the threat to the moment it had been eliminated, was over.

6.

MOZANG CHOWK, LAHORE, PAKISTAN
(January 27, 2011—Day 1)

I HAD NEVER KILLED ANYONE BEFORE. Thankfully, all ten rounds I fired found their intended targets. If my aim had been off by even just a little bit, I could have killed many more people that day.

According to the autopsy report, which showed two stick figures with Xs on them to illustrate where each man had been hit, I shot Muhammad Faheem, the man on the back of the bike, once in the left thigh, once in the right thigh, twice in the chest, and once in the back of the head. He died instantly. Faizan Haider took five rounds in the back. With its driver critically injured, the motorcycle lunged into the area between lanes where so many other motorcycles and tuk-tuks were gathered and came to a rest on its side. Haider let go of the bike, stepped over the handlebars, and tried to run away, but, as badly wounded as he was, he didn't make it very far, collapsing and dying in the median about thirty feet away from my car.

Any time lives are lost it's tragic, but I wasn't going to lose a bit of sleep over killing these two men. Once the man on the back of the motorcycle drew his gun and pointed it at me, he'd made his choice, just as I made a choice to defend myself. If someone tries to harm me, I'm going to do everything in my power to eliminate that threat, and I'll always walk away with a clear conscience because my number-one goal at the start of each of my deployments was to come home to my family. Rebecca and I now had a two-and-a-half-year-old son. I wanted nothing more than to watch him grow into a man, and I wasn't about to let anyone prevent that from happening.

As soon as I'd fired my last shot, I looked around to make sure there were no other immediate threats. I looked to the left. Nothing. To the right. Nothing. The sedan had several blind spots that obstructed my vision, so I opened my door, stepped outside, and checked my six. All clear. Then I scanned the entire area around my car one more time. Once I felt certain there weren't any more gunmen, I holstered my weapon.

A lot of people in my position would have taken off running, but with the threat eliminated I no longer felt like I was in any danger. The mood on the street was relatively calm. No one in the immediate vicinity looked as if they were even aware that shots had been fired because the sound had been mostly contained inside the sedan. Some of the motorcyclists near my car dropped their bikes and ran away when they saw the bodies and the blood. Beyond that, no one was yelling or screaming or drawing attention to the scene in any way. But I can assure you that the sense of calm that pervaded the area would have been immediately shattered if I'd bolted. Anyone who's been in Pakistan more than a day knows that if you commit any sort of public offense and try to run away, people on the street will go crazy and chase you down. The US Consulate was about three miles away from where I was, the house where I was staying about the same distance. I'd never make it that far on foot with people chasing after me.

Instead, I grabbed my camera out of my "go bag," a camera case where I stored my most essential possessions, and started taking photographs of Faheem's body. I wanted some sort of proof that showed exactly what had happened before any ambitious locals might try to clean up the scene because, as shaken by the shooting as I was, I still knew one thing: I couldn't let this turn into another Nisour Square.

THANKS TO THE RUMSFELD DOCTRINE, LOGCAP, and a 30 percent downsizing of the US military as the Cold War petered out, the use of contractors by the US military exploded in the early 1990s. At the tail end of the first Gulf War, the ratio of active-duty soldiers to private contractors in the war zone was roughly ten to one. By the end of the second Gulf War, that ratio had moved closer to even, with an estimated 100,000 contractors stationed in Iraq. In response to the insatiable demand the War on Terror had created, private military contracting mushroomed into a multibillion-dollar industry, and yet it managed to stay out of the spotlight for years. If you asked ten Americans during the first half of the 2000s to name a military contracting company, nine wouldn't have been able to come up with an answer.

The tenth would have said Blackwater.

Launched in 1997 by former Navy SEAL Erik Prince, Blackwater was named for the murky color of the North Carolina swamp that its 7,000-acre campus bordered. In the years that followed, the name would acquire an entirely new but equally gloomy connotation as the company began to make the headlines for a variety of unfortunate reasons.

On March 31, 2004, four Blackwater contractors were ambushed and killed in Fallujah, Iraq, the city just west of Baghdad that saw some of the fiercest fighting during the second Gulf War. In what would become one of the most enduring images of that entire war, a mob desecrated the bodies of the four men and hung two of them by a rope from a bridge over the Euphrates River. The families of the four men eventually opened an investigation into any wrongdoing on the part of the company, asking why there were only four men on the mission instead of the usual six and why they weren't driving armored vehicles.

For many Americans, this was the first time the military contracting industry had ever entered their consciousness, and the effect was jarring. Politicians began asking questions about the industry and the lack of oversight it enjoyed, but three months after the incident in Fallujah companies like Blackwater were actually given a Get Out of Jail Free card by Iraq's nominal head of state at the time, Paul Bremer. In one of his last acts as presidential envoy to Iraq, Bremer, who had been closely guarded by military contractors the entire fourteen months he'd served as the top US administrator in Iraq, issued Coalition Provisional Authority Order 17, granting foreign contractors immunity from Iraqi laws as long as they were working at the time of the offense. The contracting industry was further assisted in November 2006, when Defense Secretary Donald Rumsfeld, in the Pentagon's *Quadrennial Defense Review*, placed contractors under the protective umbrella of the DOD's Total Force Policy along with active and reserve military personnel.

Whatever authority Bremer and Rumsfeld had bestowed upon the industry was effectively destroyed when Blackwater made a controversial return to the headlines on September 16, 2007. Accounts vary as to what exactly transpired that day. According to the DSS spot report, four armored trucks carrying USAID officers and protected by Blackwater contractors were ambushed as they entered Baghdad's Nisour Square, a picturesque traffic circle with a fountain and statue in the center. After a VBIED detonated in the area, "an estimated 8–10 persons fired from multiple nearby locations, with some aggressors dressed in civilian apparel and others in Iraqi police uniforms. The team [of Blackwater contractors] returned defensive fire and tried to drive out of the initial ambush site."

Some witnesses, however, described a one-sided firefight, with the Blackwater contractors shooting into a crowd of innocent civilians. One of the contractors reportedly continued to shoot long after his teammates ordered him to stop firing. In the exchange, fourteen unarmed Iraqi civilians were killed, and eighteen were wounded.

In 2015, after a lengthy FBI investigation and many court battles, one of the contractors, Nicholas Slatten, was convicted of first-degree murder for his role in the affair, while three others, Paul Slough, Evan Liberty, and Dustin Heard, were found guilty of voluntary manslaughter, attempted manslaughter, and various firearms charges. While the State Department was forced to admit that "innocent life was lost," it could also boast to Iraqis that the American legal system had given them the justice that they had long demanded.

A month after the shooting at Nisour Square, the Iraqi government formally revoked the immunity from prosecution that the military contracting companies had enjoyed while operating within its borders. The incident also proved to be somewhat of a death sentence for Blackwater. On January 31, 2009, the State Department informed the company that its contract wouldn't be renewed. Blackwater subsequently changed owners and names (twice), so its current iteration, Academi, bears almost no resemblance to Erik Prince's original creation.

In the immediate aftermath of the incident at Nisour Square, it was rumored that some locals had cleaned up any shell casings that had been fired by insurgents to make it look as if the contractors hadn't been shot at and, therefore, were solely responsible for the carnage. I wasn't there, so I don't know exactly what happened that day, but I can confirm from my own experience that Islamic militants have made a point of targeting American contractors working overseas.

In the months following the 2004 Fallujah incident, Iraqi militants offered a $50,000 reward to anyone who killed a Blackwater contractor. And according to a report issued just a few months prior to my last trip to Pakistan, Lashkar-e-Taiba (LeT), a Pakistani-based terrorist group whose stated goal was to push India out of the Kashmir Valley and wage jihad against Hinduism and Judaism, had placed a similar bounty on the head of any "Blackwater operative" working in Lahore. To these groups, "Blackwater" was synonymous with *any* American military contractor. It didn't matter which company you actually worked for or what sort of work you did; if you looked like a "Blackwater operative"—American, male, in shape—they were coming after you. Does this explain what happened to me on January 27, 2011? Were Haider and Faheem LeT assassins? Maybe, maybe not. Like the country where it took place, many aspects of the incident that occurred that day remain shrouded in mystery.

What I did know for sure was that, as a military contractor, I had a target on my back. Any of the terrorist organizations that used Pakistan as a safe haven would have loved nothing more than to capture or kill me or any one of my teammates. And it wouldn't have surprised me if any of the bystanders tried to manipulate the crime scene at Mozang Chowk to make it look like I was at fault. To prevent that from happening, I took three pictures of Muhammad Faheem with my camera. I took one of his entire body slumped over the motorcycle with a gun still in his hand. Then I zoomed in and took one of his upper body so the gun was more prominent. Then I zoomed in a little bit more to show that his finger was clearly on the trigger.

Standing over his body, I could see that the gun he'd drawn was a Tokarev, a standard service pistol from the Soviet Union commonly found in Pakistan. Packing a serious punch for its size, this gun is capable of shooting through body armor. A friend of mine who works for the government and has forgotten more about weapons than I've ever known once told me, "If you ever go up against ten guys and nine of them have AKs and one has a Tokarev, you want to shoot the guy with the Tokarev first because it's one of the most dangerous weapons you're ever going to face."

In other words, Muhammad Faheem would have only needed one shot to put me down, and he'd come milliseconds away from doing just that.

AS I WAS PUTTING MY CAMERA back inside the car, the cop who'd been directing traffic walked up to me. He looked at the motorcycle and the body slumped on top of it and then at me, and he had this confused look on his face as if he wanted to ask, "What the hell happened here?"

I pulled out my black diplomatic passport and waved it in front of his face. "I'm with the US Consulate, and I need to go there right now."

It was clear by the way the traffic cop was using his hands to try to communicate with me that he didn't understand a word I'd said. I had to assume he only spoke Urdu, Pakistan's other official language besides English, or Punjabi, a regional language commonly spoken in the province we were in. I spoke neither.

I pointed at the pistol in Faheem's hand because, in my mind at least, that explained everything. The cop reached down and picked up the gun, and when the crowd forming around my car saw it, they emitted what sounded like a long collective groan as if recognizing that nothing good could come from this situation. They weren't agitated or aggressive, but from what I knew about crowds on the streets of Pakistani cities, I understood that their mood could change any second and I didn't want to be standing in the middle of them if it did.

While the traffic cop had his back to me, I got back inside the sedan and locked the doors. The relative quiet inside the car helped me calm down, and I was able to formulate a plan. I needed help. I needed to contact the consulate.

From my go bag I grabbed the two-way radio I'd been issued. "Base, this is Crossbones."

Crossbones was my call sign. Everyone on my team had one, and all of them came with a story attached. You weren't allowed to choose your own call sign; it was always given to you by one of the older guys on the team who invariably picked something that commemorated a giant fuckup you'd caused and hoped to forget. After a new guy on our team rendered one of our vehicles inoperable thanks to his overly aggressive driving, we started calling him "Axle." Another new guy kept returning to the house in vehicles that had somehow lost their bumpers, so we started calling him—you guessed it—"Bumper."

When I first arrived in Afghanistan to work on Karzai's detail in 2004, I hadn't even unpacked my clothes before an older guy with the call sign Flashlight popped his head into my room and said, "You're not bunking *here*, are you?"

"Yes, this is where they told me to go."

Flashlight was a quintessential Old Warrior. A former member of SF, he'd been in the military as far back as the Vietnam War. Now in his sixties, he didn't have even half the strength or stamina of some of the younger guys on our team, despite being in great shape, yet he was still just as effective at his job as he'd been as a twenty-year-old because his Skill Jar was full of hard-earned marbles. Any physical deficiencies he might have had, he easily made up for with his finely honed skill set and extensive range of experiences.

"Do you know the history behind this room?"

"Uh, no."

"Well," he began, propping his boot on my bed, resting an elbow on his thigh, and using his fingers to count off a list, "the first guy who lived here nearly blew off his face after accidentally discharging his weapon. He went home. The second guy fell off the side of a truck during an emergency callout, split his skull open, and nearly died. He went home. The third guy got shot in the stomach in an accident on the shooting range." He laughed and shook his head. "If you're staying in this room, you're not going to last six months. You're Crossbones, buddy."

By managing to survive in the contracting business far longer than Flashlight had predicted, I'd disproved his theory about that room, yet the name had stuck. Once you were issued a call sign, it was all but impossible to shed it, and who was going to argue with a guy like Flashlight, who'd seen and done so much over the course of his long and distinguished career? Certainly not me. I respected him implicitly and hoped to follow in his footsteps and become an Old Warrior myself one day. But sitting in my car on a street in Lahore, unsure what to do next after shooting two men, that day seemed very far away.

Snapping me out of my reverie, my radio crackled to life. "Crossbones, this is base. Go ahead."

"I was just involved in a shooting. I need you to get the guys spun up."

There was a longer than usual pause on the other end of the line. "Crossbones, could you say that again?"

"Two guys on a motorcycle pulled in front of me at an intersection. One of them drew a gun. I shot and killed both men. Things are fairly calm right now, but you're gonna want to get the guys spun up in case it goes bad."

The chief came on the line. "Where are you, Crossbones?"

"The intersection of Ferozepur Road and Jail Road."

"I need a grid."

"Roger that. Stand by." I pulled the GPS out of my bag, found the proper grid, and called it out.

"Now tell me again exactly what happened."

"I was involved in a shooting. Two men are dead. It's calm right now, but a crowd has started to form. They're not rioting or anything, but some of them don't look very happy either. I need you to get the guys ready and moving in this direction in case things go south."

NOTHING ILLUSTRATES PAKISTAN'S VOLATILITY more than the inclination on the part of its citizens to riot. If this tendency seems ingrained in their personalities, the fact that the nation grew out of the ashes of mass rioting might have something to do with it. In August 1947, the British Indian Empire split into two independent countries: Muslim-dominated Pakistan and Hindu-dominated India. The "Partition of India" turned 15 million people into refugees and millions more, who'd lived beside each other in peace for centuries, into mortal enemies. The rioting that ensued left more than a million people dead.

As awful as the violence was, it seems to have embedded itself into Pakistan's national identity somehow. The alleged theft of what was believed to be the Prophet Muhammad's hair from India's Hazratbal Shrine in 1963 kicked off riots in East Pakistan that left so many Hindus dead at the hands of angry Muslims, the incident was labeled a genocide. A false radio report that Americans had bombed the Kaaba in Mecca, the holiest site in the Islamic world, drove students in Islamabad to raid the US Embassy in 1979, nearly burning it to the ground. And the 2009 rumor that some Christians had desecrated the Koran in Gojra, a town of 150,000 in Punjab Province, inspired a mob of Muslims to torch sixty houses and kill eight people.

I really didn't want to see my name added to this list as one more victim of mob violence on a Pakistani street. For the moment, I felt safe locked inside my car, but I knew the crowd's mood could change any second, and I couldn't help thinking that if I'd been in one of our armored SUVs I wouldn't have had to be concerned about my safety at all. The crowd could have beaten on the armor until their hands were bloody, but they still wouldn't have been able to get inside.

While I was speaking with the consulate, I kept an eye on the crowd. The people milling around my car seemed more curious than anything. A few of them stood over the fallen motorcycle, pointing at Faheem's body. Others stared at me through the sedan's bullet-riddled windshield. But no one seemed too upset. They were all quite calm, not the least bit aggressive or violent.

This moment of tranquility didn't last very long. When I'd gotten out of the sedan to take photographs, I'd forgotten to put it into gear or push in the emergency brake. The car was still in neutral, and when I'd stepped out, it had rolled forward and come to rest against the car directly in front of it, with its front bumper leaning against that car's rear bumper. The two cars maintained this position until traffic began to move and the car in front of mine pulled forward. As soon as that car started moving, mine did, too, and the crowd, under the impression that I was trying to take off, that I was trying to flee the scene, went absolutely crazy.

7.

OLD ANARKALI BAZAAR, LAHORE, PAKISTAN
(January 27, 2011—Day 1)

OUR TEAM LEADER, Z, had been listening in while I was talking to the chief, and as soon as he heard what had happened at Mozang Chowk, he called Eagle Eye, one of my teammates, and told him to get moving.

Eagle Eye had been getting ready to go to the gym and stepped out of his room wearing baggy shorts and a T-shirt. "What's up?" he asked Z.

"Ray's in trouble. We need to help him out. Let's go."

They grabbed their gear, ran downstairs, and got into the SUV. Eagle Eye slid behind the wheel, and Z climbed into the passenger seat. It's hard to fault someone who's trying to help you, especially teammates who also happened to be friends, but in their eagerness to get to me Eagle Eye and Z made one crucial mistake: They didn't stop and enter my grid coordinates into their GPS while they were inside the walls of our compound where everything was calm and quiet. If they'd done that, they would have known exactly where to go. Instead they tried to do it as they were racing down the road navigating traffic, and that made what should have been a fairly routine task exponentially more difficult.

The cavalry was on its way, but it didn't know exactly where to go.

THE SENSE OF CALM EMANATING FROM the crowd hovering around my car disappeared as soon as the car in front of me drove off and my car rolled forward. Everyone started yelling at once, and a few of them began to beat on my car. One guy busted out the window on the driver-side door and reached in and tried to grab me. I managed to fight him off, but I knew that if I just stayed where I was and did nothing, the crowd, now better described as an angry mob, was going to pull me out of the car and drag me through the streets of Lahore. As worked up as they were, there was no sense in trying to appease them. I needed to get the hell out of there.

I started the sedan back up, slammed it into first gear, and, after inching my way through the crowd, started weaving through traffic, trying to put a little distance between myself and the mob. I wanted to turn left at the intersection with Ferozepur Road but couldn't. The car directly in front of me was also trying to turn left and had clogged the intersection. I had no choice but to go right.

It didn't feel like it at first, but I was making progress, slowly pulling away from the angry mob running alongside my car, when a tuk-tuk pulled in front of me and slammed on its brakes. Its driver was trying to make a U-turn to avoid a traffic jam up ahead, and when it stopped, it forced me to do the same. This allowed a motorcycle that had followed me from the site of the shooting to catch up to me. Its driver pulled right up to my rear bumper and started shouting at me in Urdu, and every time he said something it got the crowd chasing after me more worked up. With no better option available to me, I tried to push the tuk-tuk out of the way with my car, prompting its driver to shoot me a bewildered look out of his little window, but the sedan was so underpowered it barely moved it. My car's engine was whining like it was going to explode, and I couldn't help thinking, once again, how different my situation would have been if I'd been driving one of our armored SUVs. I could have simply nudged the tuk-tuk aside and been on my way.

As it was, it was a struggle. Minutes passed before I was finally able to push my way past the tuk-tuk and get back up to speed. At that point, I thought I was home free. My plan was to get on Mall Road and head straight to the consulate. I knew I'd be safe there, that I could rely on the RSO to handle the situation. But to get to Mall Road I had to navigate a series of narrow streets that were filled with as many pedestrians as vehicles. I had to constantly tap my horn just to get people to move out of the way. In the end, there were simply too many of them. For every person who moved aside, two more would suddenly appear. Most of them, it seemed, were heading to the Old Anarkali Bazaar, a busy market that was the last major obstacle between me and Mall Road. This major thoroughfare was my path to safety, and it was no more than a hundred yards away, but with so many people in my way it might as well have been a hundred miles.

I was making slow progress, foot by foot, until I came to a car idling at the edge of the market. There was a little old lady in the front seat, and a vendor from one of the shops was handing her bags of fruit and vegetables. Funneled in by the streams of pedestrians on both sides of the road, I got right behind her car and sat on my horn. The old lady looked in her rearview mirror and threw her hands up in the air as if to say, "Hey, can't you see I'm shopping here?" I might have laughed if I hadn't been so stressed out.

As I was trying to figure out what to do, the motorcycle that had been chasing me actually rammed my rear bumper. Its driver jumped off the bike and started yelling at the crowd in Urdu, whipping them into a frenzy. The crowd had swelled into the hundreds, and now that I was stopped all of them descended on my car, shaking it, hitting it, and trying to get in. One of them threw something—a rock? a brick?—at the sedan's rear window, smashing it. Adding to the chaos, Z kept calling me on the radio, but there was way too much going on for me to respond.

I decided my best chance to get away was to try to push the old lady's car out of the way, a move that might have worked if I'd been driving an SUV, but with a sedan I had very little chance. It didn't help that the street was wet and littered with food. As my wheels spun and the engine raced, all I succeeded in doing was redlining the car, and it wasn't long before the engine shut down.

As I was sitting there, one of the men in the crowd reached through the broken window on the driver-side door and started punching me. Another kicked me in the face. It was all I could do to keep them at bay, punching and kicking at their hands and pulling shut any doors they managed to open. Unless someone intervened (and quick!), I knew it wouldn't be long before one of them succeeded in getting inside the car.

Yes, I had a gun, but I wasn't about to use it. Like soldiers, contractors were required to follow very clear rules of engagement. These rules varied from country to country, with some places being much stricter than others. When I was sent on a peacekeeping mission to Macedonia in 1994 soon after joining the army, we actually had to put duct tape on our magazines. Doing this meant that in order to fire my weapon, I had to take the mag out of the gun, remove the duct tape, reinsert the mag, and chamber a round.

The rules of engagement we followed in Pakistan weren't nearly as strict. If we believed our lives were being threatened, we were authorized to use deadly force. But the moment that threat went away, we were supposed to stand down and reevaluate the scene. We couldn't just circle the wagons and shoot everything that moved. Could the mob chasing after me have killed me? Absolutely. But I wasn't about to pull out my gun and start shooting unarmed people.

Beyond the moral argument, drawing my gun would have been a bad tactical decision. With so many hands trying to grab me, it would have been extremely difficult to pull it out and use it safely. If I'd tried, someone in the crowd easily could have taken it from me and shot me with it. I'd learned this the hard way during a training session earlier in my career. Our instructors put us in various poses—standing without a weapon or lying on the ground with a gun in one hand—and we had to fight our way out of these positions against a handful of men. Doing this over and over, I learned that trying to draw a gun while getting pummeled by a crowd of people is never a good idea.

My best hope of getting out of this mess lay with the SUV heading in my direction. Z and Eagle Eye kept trying to reach me on the radio, but I was too busy fighting off people to respond. Finally, during a momentary lull in the onslaught, I grabbed the radio with one hand while using the other to fend off the crowd. "Where are you guys?"

"We're close, Crossbones. Just send us the grid, and we'll be there."

"I can't," I shouted while struggling to relock the passenger-side door. "I don't have enough hands!"

I LATER FOUND OUT that Z and Eagle Eye had problems of their own. They were racing down Jail Road when they hit a wall of traffic, created, I imagine, by the incident I'd just been involved in. During the brief conversation I'd had with Z, Eagle Eye must have heard the urgency in my voice because, instead of waiting for a break in the traffic to appear, he opted to drive over the median and against the grain of traffic on the wrong side of the road. As reckless as this might sound, from everything I've heard he wasn't going 90 mph and driving out of control. He was going maybe 30 mph, 35 tops, and he was doing his best to avoid oncoming traffic by weaving in and out and changing lanes as necessary.

At some point Eagle Eye switched tactics. Instead of constantly changing lanes, he decided to stick to a single lane, the one closest to the median, and hope any cars driving toward him in that lane would move out of the way. At first they did. The SUV was making progress, getting to within several hundred yards of where I'd been, when, with little warning, it came upon a solid line of traffic. There was a car in its lane, another car in the far left lane, and three motorcycles in the middle lane.

To avoid the oncoming car, Eagle Eye moved to the center lane, and, as he did, two of the motorcyclists hit their brakes and veered behind the cars in the outer lanes. But the third motorcyclist, a cosmetics trader named Ibad-ur Rehman, never saw the SUV barreling down on him. Having just passed Mozang Chowk, he was looking over his shoulder at the crowd still lingering around the spot where the shooting had taken place. Eagle Eye slammed on the brakes, nearly coming to a complete stop, but Rehman was at full throttle when he hit the vehicle head-on.

Blood splattered the SUV's windshield and hood.

WITH THE CROWD SECONDS AWAY from getting into the sedan, my situation was getting desperate. They continued to grab me and punch me through the busted window. After one of them opened the passenger door, I reached over and grabbed the door handle and tried to pull it closed. Hands and fingers were in the way, but I didn't care. I crunched them with the door. When I finally got the door closed, I locked it, but by that time someone else in the crowd had succeeded in opening one of the rear doors, and I had to start the whole process over again. This went on I don't know how many times. It was like playing whack-a-mole; every time I succeeded in closing and locking one door, another one would fly open. At this rate, I knew it was only a matter of time before the crowd managed to pull me out of the car.

Fortunately, a traffic cop on a motorcycle intervened. My situation was way above this guy's pay grade, but I was still happy to see him. During all this confusion the little old lady in the car in front of me had managed to drive away, so the cop was able to park his motorcycle right in front of my car. Placing himself in between the crowd and my car, he did his best to prevent people from hitting me. He fought them off and pushed them out of the way, giving me a momentary reprieve. He also managed to reach inside the car, pull my keys out of the ignition, and pocket them. I wasn't going anywhere now.

Upset that he was helping me, the crowd yelled at the cop in Urdu, and he yelled back at them in English. "Are you people mad? This man still has a gun!"

His words hardly fazed the crowd, but the arrival of two Punjabi Rangers had a more pronounced effect, perhaps because they are an elite paramilitary outfit and carry guns. Despite the respect they're given as soldiers, they're still best known for the part they play in the "retreat ceremony" performed every evening in Wagah, a border town on the only motorway—the famed Grand Trunk Road—that connects Pakistan with its most reviled enemy, India. For forty-five theatrical minutes, members of the Rangers and the Indian Border Security Force mimic each other's actions, goose-stepping, high-kicking, stamping their feet, and glaring at each other across the border. This daily ritual ends with the setting of the sun, the shaking of hands, the lowering of both countries' flags, and the slamming of the border gates.

Beyond their role in this well-choreographed drama, the Rangers are responsible for maintaining law and order in Pakistan's biggest cities, and they're very good at their jobs, so it didn't surprise me all that much when one of them succeeded in fighting his way through the crowd and getting into the passenger seat of my car. I looked at him, and he looked at me, both of us not quite sure how to proceed.

Having an armed police officer in the car with me raised the stakes of the game I was caught up in. I reminded myself to go slow, be smart, and not overreact to anything. Good advice, as it turned out, because the first thing he did was pull out his pistol. I waited to see what he was going to do with it. Fortunately, he didn't point it at me. He simply laid it in his lap and with his other hand made a gesture as if to say, "Trust me. Everything's going to be all right."

We continued to stare at each other, barely breathing, until an older Punjabi Ranger, who I assumed by his authoritative demeanor was the younger one's boss, climbed into the back seat of the sedan. With two police officers now in the car, I was growing resigned to my fate; they were now in charge of the situation, a power shift that only grew clearer when the young Ranger raised his gun up to the window and barked a command in Urdu. With that, the crowd jumped back, just as he'd intended.

I had no idea what caused it or what it meant, but a change soon came over the crowd. It went from being completely out of control, with people yelling all sorts of different things, to eerily focused, with them swaying in rhythm together and chanting the same thing over and over. I initially thought this was a positive development, but the traffic cop, who'd been guarding my door this entire time, set me straight. He stuck his head into the car and said, "My name is Muhammad. I want to help you. We have to get you out of here right now. These people want to kill you."

He looked genuinely scared, which made his report seem credible. "All right," I told him. "Sounds good."

"You're going to have to trust me. I need you to give me your gun. Don't worry. We're going to protect you."

"Do I have your word on that?"

"Yes. Of course. We're the police. Now give me your gun."

"Okay, but I'm not going to be the one to pull it out. I don't want to make these people any madder than they already are." I took his hand, and I placed it on my gun. "Here it is. Take it."

Muhammad grabbed my gun and pulled it out of the car. He removed the magazine and put it in one of his sweater pockets, then racked the gun and cleared the chamber. As he stepped away from the car with my gun in his hand, the crowd surged forward to fill the vacuum.

"Muhammad, where are you going?" I yelled.

He didn't answer, just kept walking.

I thought he'd tricked me, that he'd said to the crowd something to the effect of, "I've got his gun now. Go get him," and that infuriated me. "Muhammad, you motherfucker!" I yelled at his back. "You promised!"

The crowd resumed beating on the car and trying to pull me out. With the Punjabi Rangers doing little to stop them, I knew it was up to me to defend myself, and I fought back with everything I had. I no longer held myself in check. I was punching people in the head and using the doors to crush their fingers, figuring if I was going down, I was going to take as many of these people with me as I could.

AFTER HITTING THE MOTORCYCLIST, the SUV came to a stop, backed up, drove around the crumpled motorcycle and Ibad-ur Rehman's body, then continued moving forward until it reached the intersection where the shooting had occurred. Hundreds of people had witnessed the SUV's collision with the motorcycle, and many of them had chased after the vehicle on foot after it drove off. When the SUV arrived at Mozang Chowk, it brought this new crowd with it, nearly doubling the number of irate people in the area.

Z got on the radio and called base. "We see where the incident occurred, but we can't see Ray. We can't even see his car. It's hard to tell what's going on. The crowd's too big."

As Z and Eagle Eye were scanning the area for me, a man from the crowd yanked open the SUV's driver-side door. Eagle Eye responded by flashing his pistol in an effort to ward off the man and any others who dared come close, while shouting, "Get back! Get back!" As soon as he was able to, Eagle Eye slammed the door shut and locked it. When someone else from the crowd managed to open Z's door, he used his rifle to the same effect.

Z radioed base. "We can't stay here. There are too many people in the area, and they're all worked up. They're trying to pull us out of our vehicle."

While he was talking, a police car pulled in front of the SUV, trying to box it in and prevent it from leaving.

"Now the police have arrived. It looks like they're going to try to detain us."

There was a brief moment of silence on the other end of the line as the chief debated how to proceed. "Abort the mission. Do you understand? Get out of there right now."

And so they did. Unable to move forward, they drove down the street in reverse and got off the main road at the first available opportunity. They took a series of access roads northwest, then headed east for a bit, before driving south back into the city. They were followed by the local police the entire way but were able to make it to the consulate without getting stopped and left the country.

And with them went my best chance of getting out of this mess.

8.

OLD ANARKALI POLICE STATION, LAHORE, PAKISTAN
(January 27, 2011—Day 1)

As it turned out, my anger directed at Muhammad, the traffic cop, had been misplaced. He'd walked away only to put my gun in a secure place. When he made it back to my car, he opened my door, pushed me toward the center console, and climbed in. Using the keys he'd removed from the ignition and pocketed earlier, he started the car and drove me and the two Punjabi Rangers to the Old Anarkali Police Station just down the street from where I'd been stopped.

Muhammad and the Rangers led me to a room inside the station that was crowded with police officers talking excitedly in a mix of Urdu, English, and Punjabi. The most important thing for me to do at this point, I knew, was get in touch with the RSO. Fixing messes like the one I was currently involved in was precisely what the RSO did.

I pulled the lanyard I was wearing around my neck from beneath my flannel shirt and pointed at my identification badges. "I need to tell the embassy where I'm at."

One of the officers grabbed my set of badges and studied it. "You're from America?"

"Yes."

"You belong to the American Embassy?"

I knew my exact status was going to be difficult to explain. I hoped showing him my badges and passport and visa would be enough. "Yes, but my passport—"

One of the other officers in the room pointed at my name on one of the badges. "Raymond?"

Ignoring him, I continued speaking with the first officer. "—is at the site I showed the police officer. It's somewhere. It's lost."

There must have been a dozen officers in the room, and all of them were talking at once, and I could barely understand a word of it.

The officer studied the badges around my neck. "Who do you work for? The ambassador?"

"The consulate general. It's—not an ambassador. In here, Lahore. Yes." I pointed at one of my badges. "This is an old badge. This is Islamabad." I showed him another one. "This is Lahore."

"You are now working in Lahore?"

"Yes."

"As a . . . ?"

I had a feeling it wouldn't be a good idea to mention the exact nature of my work. As a security contractor, it wasn't like I was involved in any sort of clandestine operations. "I just work as a consultant there."

"Consultant?"

"Yeah."

"And what is your name?"

"Raymond Davis."

Two or three of the officers repeated my name while some of the other officers continued a conversation that was so loud it threatened to drown out everything else. It obviously wasn't as chaotic in that room as it had been out on the street, but it wasn't that much more peaceful, either.

I took a deep breath. "Can I sit down?"

"Please do," said one of the officers. "Give you water?"

I took a seat in the chair that was offered to me and recalled one of the golden rules tourists must abide by in Pakistan: Unless you're looking to pick up a nasty stomach virus, you'd be wise to avoid drinking the tap water. "Do you have a bottle?"

He looked at me blankly.

"A bottle of water."

His expression—oblivious, confused—didn't change.

I made a drinking gesture with my hand. "Bottled water."

Finally understanding me, he joked, "No money, no pani." Pani was one of the few Urdu words I knew. It meant water.

Several of the officers laughed, but I wasn't in the mood to join them. "Can you search the car for my passport?"

They did, and when they returned they had it, as well as my go bag. They took everything out of the bag, laid all my possessions onto a table, and started rifling through them, picking up each item and presenting it to me.

"Is this yours?"

"Yes."

"Is this yours?"

"Yes."

"Is this yours?"

"Yes."

One of the officers took my cell phone and stuck it in my shirt pocket, while another officer shoved all my gear back into my bag and handed it to me.

"Come with us. We have to get you out of here. It's too dangerous here. We have to take you somewhere safe."

They put a blanket over my head and led me out of the building. It was quiet outside. Which meant the angry mob hadn't followed me here. Which meant what the officers had said about me not being safe didn't add up. They were lying.

The officers hustled me into a vehicle, which immediately took off down the road. I had a good idea what was happening. I was pretty sure they were taking me to Cantonment, a military base on the east side of Lahore out near the airport, where the consulate's RSO would have a much more difficult time finding me.

Using the blanket as cover, I fished my cell phone out of my shirt pocket and fired off a text to the last person I'd called, a guy on my team we called Goose.

"They're taking me to Cantt. Tell the RSO."

I WAS RIGHT. When the vehicle stopped and the blanket was removed from my head, I saw we were on a military base. I would have felt right at home if we'd been in the United States, but, this being Pakistan, I was concerned.

While Pakistan is said to be a parliamentary federal republic with a president who serves as head of state and a prime minister who runs the government, everyone knows the real power in that country lies with the military. For more than half of the sixty-four years that had passed since its birth as a nation, Pakistan had been under military rule. It devoted nearly a quarter of its budget to defense spending. As recently as 2007, Pakistan had been under martial law. That same year, President Pervez Musharraf, a former four-star general, suspended the constitution, had the leader of the opposition party arrested, and dismissed the Supreme Court's chief justice. In short, you didn't want to cross the military in Pakistan.

With its manicured lawns and freshly painted buildings, the military base I was taken to could have passed for an idyllic country estate, and yet it felt as if I were being pulled into some dark hole. Two guards escorted me into one of the buildings, down a long hallway, and into a room where a handful of officers were present. One of the officers, an extremely young-looking lieutenant, was sitting on a bed shoved against the wall in one corner of the room. Two other officers were sitting behind a desk. There was one other desk in the room, and another officer was sitting behind it. I was directed to a chair on the opposite side of the desk from him. The guard who was carrying my bag set it on a chair behind me, took my cell phone out of my shirt pocket, and placed it on the desk.

The officer on the other side of the desk gave me a sympathetic smile. "You have had a difficult day. Those two men were very bad men. We understand you had to protect yourself. They had guns. They had ammunition. They were looking to hurt you."

I nodded in agreement.

"You, sir, are very good shooter. You are very well trained."

"I'm okay, I guess."

"How often do you shoot?"

"I shoot once a year for quals."

The way he looked at me, it was clear he didn't understand.

"Firearms requalification training," I explained. "We do it once a year."

He shook his head and chuckled. "No, sir, you shoot more than once a year. We know. You must shoot all the time."

I shrugged.

"I saw the shots. You are very good shooter. We could use you to train our police."

I wasn't sure if he was joking or not. Up until this point in my life, I'd never been in any sort of trouble with the law, but I knew that, in the United States at least, if you committed a crime, you either paid a fine, went to jail, did community service, or completed some combination of the three. I didn't know much about Pakistani law, but it seemed as if the officer was suggesting that I teach some of his men how to shoot as some sort of community service. The idea didn't sit well with me, but I chose not to say anything about it.

"The shots were expertly placed. They—" His phone rang, and he stood up from his chair to take the call.

Another officer took his place. "Okay," he said, "tell me what happened."

I cleared my throat. "I was at the intersection of Jail Road and Ferozepur Road. I was just sitting there in traffic when I looked up and—"

When his phone rang, he stood up to answer it.

Another officer walked over and sat on the edge of the desk. "Go on. Tell me what happened. From the beginning."

"I was at the intersection of—"

"No, no, no. Where were you coming from?"

I wasn't about to compromise the safety of my team by telling him where our house was located. "I was coming from the consulate, and when I got to the intersection of—"

"What were you doing driving around? Where were you going?"

He was fishing for information that had nothing to do with the incident, and I wasn't about to give him anything that could get one of my teammates hurt or killed. "I was going to that restaurant in the old part of Lahore that has such great views. You know, the Cuckoo's Nest."

The young-looking lieutenant who'd been sitting on the bed stood up and walked over to me. "How do you know about the Cuckoo's Nest?" he asked. His English was almost perfect, and, to be honest, he seemed like one of the brighter guys in the room, but the officer who'd started to question me shooed him away.

"The Cuckoo's Nest, huh?" he said. "How do you know about this place?"

"I heard it's a good place to eat. I read about it in a guidebook."

"And what were you—"

Then *his* phone rang. This kept happening. Every time one of the officers in the room asked me a question and I started to answer it, he'd get a phone call from someone asking about the incident, and I'd get cut off. It was a little annoying, but having to go back and tell my story from the very beginning each time I got interrupted actually worked to my benefit. I'd been told that, if I were ever to find myself in this sort of situation, I should delay giving information as much as possible while waiting for the RSO to show up. Knowing that every minute that passed gave the RSO that much more time to find me, I was more than happy to sit there and tell the same story over and over again.

What quickly became apparent was that the officers interrogating me didn't care all that much about the actual details of the shooting or the identities of the two dead men. They were far more interested in *me*. They wanted to know exactly who I was and what I was doing in Lahore. Other than the part about driving from the consulate to the Cuckoo's Nest, I told the truth. I didn't make stuff up. But I wasn't volunteering to give them any information, either. They would have to beat it out of me, particularly anything that had to do with my team and the house where we were staying. As far as I was concerned, I was solely responsible for the shooting. I wasn't going to drag anyone else into this mess. In my head at least, my teammates didn't even exist.

What also became clear after several hours of questioning continually interrupted by phone calls was that these officers weren't very skilled at interrogation. While I'd never actually interrogated someone myself, I did know a thing or two about getting information from people. When I was studying at Eastern Kentucky University, I worked part-time as a loss-prevention detective at the T. J. Maxx in Lexington. A big part of the job was interviewing people who'd been caught stealing from the store, and I read a lot of books on the subject, including such classics as *Essentials of the Reid Technique: Criminal Interrogation and Confessions* and *Practical Aspects of Interview and Interrogation*. From these books, I learned the difference between "soft-sell" (using kind words and gestures to build a rapport in hopes the person being questioned will start talking voluntarily) and "hard-sell" (basically, beating the crap out of someone). At T. J. Maxx, I stuck strictly to the soft-sell. Using that technique, I once got someone to confess to stealing more than $100,000 worth of merchandise from the store over the course of several months. The soft-sell was extremely effective if done properly, but none of the officers who questioned me knew how to do it. They failed to understand the importance of building a rapport before attempting to get the information they sought.

I was also surprised when, after I'd asked if I could use my phone, they said yes.

I called Goose. "Did you get my message?"

"Yeah, Crossbones, I told the RSO you're in Cantonment. Everyone's running around trying to figure out what to do. Don't worry. We're on it."

"Good. Thanks."

"One thing that came up—do you have access to your GPS?"

I glanced over my shoulder at my bag, which was sitting on the chair behind me. "Possibly."

"Do you remember how to zero it out?"

"I believe so, yes."

"Well, let me walk you through it real quick just in case."

He didn't need to explain why it was so important for me to delete all the data stored in my GPS. It contained a detailed history of my movements in Lahore as well as that of any contractors who'd used it before me. The route I'd driven that morning was the same route we were supposed to take someone on three days later. If these officers obtained that information, that mission would be compromised.

The GPS also contained plenty of trivial information as well, such as trips to the consulate to mail a package or to a local hotel to get a haircut, but, as inconsequential as that information might have seemed, it still qualified as intelligence. And with the below-the-radar game constantly being played by Pakistan's powerful spy agency, the Inter-Services Intelligence (ISI), I didn't want any information their hands.

After Goose reminded me how to delete all the information stored on my GPS and did his best to inject a little humor into a very stressful situation—"Don't forget to keep your cheeks together, brother!"—I asked one of the officers in the room if I could get the can of dip I kept in my bag.

He looked at me like he had no idea what I was talking about.

"Copenhagen," I said. "You know, chewing tobacco."

He shook his head to show he still didn't understand.

"*Naswar*," I said, pointing to my bag.

Similar to *khat* and coca, *naswar* is a plant-based drug that produces a mild high. It is used in much the same way as chewing tobacco or snuff and is especially popular—one could go so far as to say culturally ingrained—among the Pashtun people of Pakistan and Afghanistan.

"*Naswar*? I see. Yes, go on. Get it."

I turned around and started rifling through my bag, while using my body to hide what I was doing. My tin of Copenhagen was sitting on top of all the other stuff in the bag, but I pushed it aside and started fiddling with the GPS. According to Goose's instructions, I needed to turn the power off before I could erase the data. I shut it down, then started hitting the buttons in the order he'd told me to, but with my hands inside the bag and my body turned, it must have been obvious that I was up to something. **Do You Want to Delete All?** appeared on the screen, and I was just about to hit **Yes** when the young lieutenant walked over, snatched the GPS out of my hand, and held it up for the other officers to see.

This caused a huge uproar in the room, with all the officers speaking at once, as if they were haggling over the price of a rug at a street bazaar instead of conducting a formal interrogation. They continued shouting over each other's heads until a man in a suit stepped into the room. Upon seeing him, everyone in the room fell silent like a bunch of elementary school kids on those rare occasions when the principal pays a visit to their classroom.

Seemingly oblivious to the respect being paid to him, the man in the suit took a seat on the other side of the desk from me, while continuing to smoke a cigarette and talk on his phone. The way the air inside the room had changed once this man walked in, I knew without asking who he was and which organization he worked for. ISI was now involved, which meant whatever hole I was in had just gotten a lot deeper.

9.

US EMBASSY, ISLAMABAD, PAKISTAN
(January 27, 2011—Day 1)

C AMERON MUNTER, then US Ambassador to Pakistan, understood the importance of working with, not against, ISI to resolve the predicament I was in. He was a career diplomat who'd risen up the ranks of the Foreign Service to become deputy chief of mission in the Czech Republic, Poland, and Iraq, as well as ambassador to Serbia, before arriving at Islamabad three months before the shooting.

Munter first became aware of the incident when he saw footage of it playing on a twenty-four-hour English-language news channel on a television in his office. At first he had far more questions than answers, but two things immediately seemed clear to the ambassador. First, television interviews with people who said the men I'd shot had robbed them earlier in the day indicated that the men were common thieves who simply ended up in the wrong place at the wrong time; and, second, the only thing that really mattered, as far as he was concerned, was whether or not I had diplomatic status.

Once it was established that I had a diplomatic passport, Munter, while meeting with his Country Team, suggested that he reach out to the Pakistani authorities with a *mea culpa*. He saw no downside in taking responsibility for what had happened because, as a diplomat, he understood that it really didn't matter what I'd done. As long as I was attached to the US Embassy, I was protected by diplomatic immunity.

"We have to go to the Pakistani authorities," Munter said in the meeting. "We need to say, 'This is our guy. This is a terrible thing that's happened, but you have no jurisdiction over him. You need to release him.'"

IN THIS WAY, the US Embassy in Pakistan was not unlike ISI, a large bureaucracy whose many divisions rarely worked in conjunction with each other. All too often one division of ISI would profess to be working toward one goal, while another one of its divisions would be operating in a manner that seemed in direct opposition to the other's efforts.

With President Obama's backing, the US government began to increase its presence in Pakistan. This expansion, when combined with the influx of American aid workers as part of the Enhanced Partnership with Pakistan Act, a nonmilitary aid package that promised to give Pakistan $1.5 billion per year from 2010 to 2014, helped turn the US Embassy in Islamabad into one of the most heavily populated missions in the world, with an estimated 2,500 people working there. So many new employees were arriving at the embassy each day that when Ambassador Munter arrived there in October 2010, some staff members were actually working at desks in the hallways.

In such a chaotic atmosphere, it was almost inevitable that mistakes would be made. Munter admitted as much in a 2015 interview. "I think the embassy—the State Department management people who were in charge of keeping the diplomatic status lists up to date—I think we just missed a couple signals. We were trying to build the relationship between the two countries, build the number of diplomats who were there, and we didn't keep up with the paperwork very well. We didn't keep our records straight. We got caught up in that big expansion of relations, and we were sloppy in our recordkeeping."

One of those slip-ups involved me. Apparently, my name was left off a list showing which Americans within Pakistan had received the proper diplomatic accreditation. It was nothing more than a small clerical error, but, when combined with several other blunders that seemed equally harmless at the time, it would turn out to have very serious consequences.

10.

LAHORE CANTONMENT, LAHORE, PAKISTAN
(January 27, 2011—Day 1)

T HE ROOM WHERE I WAS BEING HELD in Cantonment seemed much smaller after the man in the suit entered it. He walked over and leaned against the edge of the desk I was sitting at, but he didn't look at me, didn't acknowledge me in any way, just continued to talk on his phone and smoke his cigarette as if he had all the time in the world. It was a power play, and everyone in the room went right along with it, refusing to say a word. When he finally put down his phone and stubbed out his cigarette, he studied me for a long time as if trying to guess how much I weighed.

"Tell me what happened."

I wasn't talking until I knew who I was talking to. "Excuse me. Who are you?"

"I'm the Colonel."

Because I was in Cantonment, I assumed that meant he was a colonel in the military police. But he hadn't answered my question, not really, so I pressed him. "I'm sorry, Colonel *who?*"

"I'm the Colonel," he repeated.

If I had any doubts about the man's identity, they disappeared with this lame attempt at deception. My initial instinct, that he worked for ISI, seemed accurate.

The Colonel lit a fresh cigarette and pointed it at me. "You must have quite a story to tell. Please share it with me."

I started telling him my account of what had happened at Mozang Chowk, and unlike the other officers, he actually let me tell my story

without interrupting me. I gave the short version, and when I came to
the end he nodded and asked, "Where do you work?"

"The US Consulate."

"Which office?"

I repeated what I'd said earlier. "The RAO. The Regional Affairs
Office."

"I see. All right, who's the RSO?"

"Bill Womack," I said with great confidence.

The Colonel raised an eyebrow. "He just left. Who's the *new* RSO?"

Oof. Whenever I arrived in country on a new contract, I would usually head straight to the embassy or consulate to meet everyone. Well, I
hadn't done that on this trip. As soon as I'd arrived in Lahore, I got right
to work, and during the six days that had passed I just never got around
to visiting the consulate. I'd heard that Bill Womack had cycled out and
that there was a new RSO, but I never got his name. Not knowing this
piece of information flustered me a little.

The Colonel tried to take advantage, abruptly switching topics. "Who
were the men coming after you?"

His question seemed to come out of nowhere, and I told him as much.
"I don't know anyone who was coming after me."

"Yes, you do. You talked to them on your radio."

"No, when I used my radio, I was talking to the consulate, telling
them what had happened."

"Some men came after you. We know this. Who were they?"

"I don't know what you're talking about."

"Very well." The Colonel took a drag off his cigarette and exhaled just
above my head. "Then tell me about the motorcycle you hit."

"What? I hit a motorcycle?"

"Yes. When did you hit the motorcycle?"

"I hit a motorcycle?"

It was at this point in the conversation that I began to suspect that
the Colonel was trying to reprise the interrogation tactics used by Sheriff
Farley in *My Cousin Vinny*. While questioning Bill Gambini, played by a
young Ralph Macchio, the sheriff asks, "When did you shoot the clerk?"
to which Gambini responds with a question of his own: "I shot the clerk?"
Later, while the sheriff is reading the transcript of the interrogation in

court, he makes Gambini's question sound more like a declarative sentence and therefore a confession: "I shot the clerk."

I had a feeling that the same thing was going on here. The Colonel was trying to trap me into "confessing" that I'd hit a motorcycle, to tie me to a death I could somehow be blamed for instead of the two that had resulted from a clear act of self-defense, so when he said, "Yes, you hit a motorcycle with your SUV," I was happy to correct him.

"No, no, no. I wasn't driving an SUV. I was driving a white sedan."

The Colonel turned to one of the officers in the room and asked him a question in Urdu. This is what the conversation sounded like to me:

"Blah blah blah jibber jabber white sedan?"

To which the officer responded, "Blah blah blah jibber jabber white sedan."

When they were done, the Colonel turned to me. "It appears that it was *your friends* who hit the motorcyclist and killed him." He jabbed his cigarette at me. "But *you* are going to be the one held responsible for that."

Up to this point I thought that the police had been doing their best to properly investigate the incident, that they wanted to do the right thing, but after what the Colonel had just said, any warm feelings I'd had disappeared. His words were like a slap in the face. I suddenly realized just how hard ISI was willing to press me and just how little power I had to stop them.

I looked at the Colonel incredulously. "You know what? I'm finished talking here. That's it. You're not getting another word out of me. I'm done."

SEVERAL HOURS LATER—I don't know exactly how long because my watch and phone had been confiscated—the young lieutenant brought me a sheet of paper and a pen and told me to write down everything that had happened to me that day. I was happy to do it. I spent hours and hours working on my statement because I wanted to make sure I got it exactly right. Guards kept coming into the room, asking me if I was done yet, but I refused to let them rush me. I took my time, remembering to include every single word of my story, exactly the way I'd told it earlier in the day. The only information I left out was where I'd come from and where I was going.

But, of course, that's what the officers were most interested in. After looking over my statement, they bombarded me with questions. "What were you doing in that neighborhood? Where were you going? Who were the guys who came after you in the SUV?" And on and on.

"Look," I said, "I already told you. I'm done answering questions. Everything you need to know is in that statement. I'm not talking anymore."

It took several more rounds of them asking a question and my refusing to answer it before they finally got it: They weren't getting anything out of me. This took a while, though. By the time they led me to the room where I was to be held that night, it was late. Thanks to all the drama I'd witnessed that day, I wasn't tired. The atmosphere inside that room didn't exactly promote relaxation, either. As in the previous room, this one contained a television that seemed to be stuck on coverage of the incident. It was the lead story and the second story and the third. I saw angry protesters burning tires at the site of the shooting. I saw even angrier protestors holding signs and chanting. I was effectively being tried by the Pakistani media, and from the tone of the commentators' voices, the verdict wasn't in my favor. I desperately needed help, but the RSO—or anyone from the consulate for that matter—was still nowhere in sight.

Adding to my stress, four guards were in the room with me at all times, two of them sitting in chairs on either side of the door and two sitting on the bed on the other side of the room. I sat on a bed opposite theirs with my head resting against the cold stone wall, and I pulled the blanket up so that I was covered but could still see what was going on in the room because I didn't like being outnumbered four to one. I could tell from the television coverage that a lot of people in Pakistan were extremely upset about the incident. If the guards were to kill me, they'd probably come off looking like heroes—and if they did try to attack me, what could I do?

At one point during the night, two of the guards started pointing at the TV, then at me, in a way that made it clear they were talking about what had happened earlier in the day, and they sounded angry. This was fairly unnerving, but it wasn't even half as alarming as the moment when three of the guards stood up and walked out of the room, and, as soon as they were gone, the one they'd left behind took his gun out of its holster.

With that, all kinds of thoughts went careening through my brain, but the most persistent and convincing one was that he was going to shoot me. I tried to stay calm and think through the best way to respond if the guard raised his gun and aimed it at me. He was standing at least seven or eight feet away from me, too far for me to lunge at him, grab the gun, and take it away from him. Even if I succeeded, I'd still be stuck inside a police station that was crawling with armed guards. Another but no more appealing option was to turn around and let him shoot me in the back. That way, it would be obvious that he'd executed a defenseless person.

Before letting my thoughts spiral out of control, I put myself in his shoes for a second. He was the size of a jockey, and he'd been left all alone in a room with a guy nearly twice as big as he was. I weighed 255 pounds at the time and could push-press that same amount over my head multiple times. If you added my imposing physique with my somewhat terrifying image—the police were trying to make me look like some kind of highly trained assassin—the poor guy was probably just scared out of his mind. By pulling out his gun, he may only have been trying to protect himself in case I tried to attack him.

The mystery surrounding his intentions only deepened when he heard the other three guards walking down the hall on their way back to the room and he scrambled to reholster his gun and sit back down before they entered. By the time they opened the door, he had his hands in his lap and was looking up at the TV as if he'd been watching it the entire time they'd been gone and didn't have a care in the world. But it was obvious, to me at least, that he was hiding something from the other guards. Was it the fact that he'd been scared or that he'd been planning on shooting me? I didn't know. But either way, one thing was clear.

I couldn't trust anyone.

11.

HIGHLANDS RANCH, COLORADO
(January 27, 2011—Day 1)

I HEARD ABOUT THE INCIDENT THE DAY OF. *It was in the morning, about ten-ish. Maybe 10:15, 10:20. I was paying bills and watching* Grey's Anatomy *on Hulu, and I got a phone call from Ron, one of Ray's supervisors.*

"There was an incident this morning," he said. "I wanted you to hear it from me first. Two guys tried to rob Ray."

I didn't know what to say, and when I don't know what to say I get nervous, and when I get nervous sometimes I act awkwardly. I knew Ron was expecting me to respond like an emotional woman, like some hysterical housewife, but that was not how I felt. Instead, I laughed. I don't know why I thought it was funny. I just did. The idea of someone trying to rob Ray just seemed so absurd to me. He was the last *person on earth you'd want to rob. Not that he was dangerous or anything. He was just a really big guy with a whole bunch of training. Trying to rob him would be like trying to take food from a grizzly bear—not a good idea.*

Exhaustion probably contributed to my dark humor. With Ray gone all the time, I'd pretty much raised our son all by myself from the time he was four months old, and I still hadn't caught up on my sleep. Our son was born with some health issues that required me to constantly shuttle him to and from the doctor. One time while I was driving him to one of his appointments, I actually started hallucinating in the car. That's how tired I was. It was bad. Laughing at stuff, even when it might seem strange to others, helped me get through some difficult times.

Long before the incident in Pakistan, I learned how to turn my feelings off like a light switch. Don't get me wrong. I'm a sensitive person—some would even go so far as to say overly sensitive—but when certain situations get too intense I tend to turn off that switch. It's much easier for me to act strong and take care of others than it is for me to let my guard down and be vulnerable.

Ron probably thought I'd lost my mind, but he never stopped talking. He told me as much about the incident as he could, given the lack of information available. From what he'd been told, Ray had been robbed, but that story didn't make much sense to me.

"Who would be dumb enough to try to rob Ray?" I said. "I feel kinda sorry for them. I hope they're still walking."

"Well, actually, they're both dead," Ron said.

"What? Oh my god! Is Ray all right?"

"Ray's fine. Not a scratch on him. But he's been detained. From what I can tell Ray was just defending himself, but the police still need to question him. According to the first report I got, he should be out within six hours. I promise you everything's going to be fine. Ray's a big boy. You don't need to worry about him."

I'D NEVER SPENT MUCH TIME WORRYING ABOUT RAY. All the training I'd received while I was in the army helped me keep things in perspective. Due to the nature of his job, I also knew he couldn't check in with me every single day, so I never came to expect that. As a security contractor, he didn't have the same access to communications equipment as he would have if he'd been in the military. If he'd been in the army, he would have been able to use a computer or phone whenever he got back from one of his missions. For example, Bagram Airfield in Afghanistan actually has several computer centers where soldiers can get on the Internet and make free phone calls any time of day.

As a contractor, Ray didn't have that. His team usually had access to a satellite phone, but he couldn't use it for more than about five minutes or so at a time. The first year he was away, we got our own sat phone, but, at $3 a minute, we quickly realized it was a luxury we really couldn't afford. During the first nine months we had it, we spent $3,000 on phone bills! We tried communicating more by email, but if Ray wasn't near a computer it could be a really long time before I got a response. It wasn't unusual for us to go weeks without talking to each other, which was really hard, especially when you have a toddler who is sick all the time.

When I didn't hear from Ray for a while, I had to remind myself not to worry about him. I would tell myself that if something bad had happened to him, someone would have called me and told me about it. That's where my time in the army really helped. Other people might have gotten anxious and scared, but I was able to comfort myself knowing that Ray had been trained to handle nearly every single situation you could possibly think of. For me to be able to sleep at night, I simply had to trust his judgment and believe he was making smart decisions and not putting himself at risk any more than he needed to. Once I'd mastered that little mental trick, I didn't spend a whole lot of time worrying about him. Over the years, I'd grown comfortable knowing that Ray could handle himself just fine. I just needed him to come home when he was supposed to, and he always did.

That evening, one of Ray's colleagues, a guy named TK, showed up at my door. TK was a great guy and incredibly dedicated to his job. How dedicated? His wife had just had a baby, and here he was at my front door, offering to help me any way he could. After he showed me his ID and badge, I invited him in and we sat down and talked. He seemed a little nervous at first, but after we'd chatted for a while, he began to visibly relax.

"Phew," he said. "Thank god. I thought you were going to be an emotional wreck, and, as many dicey situations as I've been trained to deal with, comforting a hysterical wife isn't one of them."

I laughed. "No, everything's going to be just fine. I'm sure of it."

He grinned and shook his head. "I'm so glad you've got such a positive attitude. Most people in your shoes would be falling apart, and, honestly, I'm not sure how I would have handled that."

I laughed again. This seemed like a much healthier reaction to me than melting into a blubbering mess. The entire situation was just so surreal. It was hard to get my head around it. I felt like I was in The Twilight Zone or something. It wasn't that I wasn't taking the situation seriously, I just wasn't overly concerned. Like Ron, TK assured me that Ray would be out soon, so I had nothing to worry about, right?

RON CALLED ME FIRST THING IN THE MORNING, just like he'd said he would. "The situation over there is turning out to be a little more complicated than we'd first thought. But please don't worry. We just have to manage a few things. Ray should be out soon. By the end of the day at the very latest."

"Can you tell me how he is? How's he holding up?"

"He's good. He's fine. He's being held for questioning. We're doing our best to get him out. It's just taking a little longer than we'd anticipated."

"They're not beating him or anything, are they?"

"That's the first thing we're going to ask him. I promise you."

"You mean, you-all haven't seen him yet?"

"No, it took longer than expected to locate him. They moved him to a military base. A team from the consulate will be meeting with him later today."

"Well, please tell them to check every inch of Ray's body to make sure he's not getting beaten. Because even if he had three cracked ribs and a busted nose, Ray wouldn't say anything. He doesn't like to admit when he's in pain."

"That's good to know. I'll be sure to pass that along."

Despite his assurances, I didn't feel like Ron was taking what I'd said seriously enough. To drive home the point, I told him about the time Ray got sick and had to go to the hospital and the nurse didn't put his IV in correctly.

"That looks really painful," I'd said to Ray, pointing at his arm, which had grown red and swollen.

He shrugged. "Eh, it's a little uncomfortable."

"Well, let's have the nurse come take it out and put it in right."

"It's really not a big deal."

"What do you mean it's no big deal? Your arm looks awful."

It really did. It was turning purple, and I could tell by the look on his face that he was in a lot of pain, even though he wouldn't admit it. I hit the call button and asked the nurse to come take a look at it ASAP. When she pulled back the bandage, it became clear there was a problem with the way the catheter had been put in. No fluid was flowing through the tube. I'm not even sure the nurse had found a vein.

"Oh my goodness," she said, "we're going to have to redo this. I'm so sorry."

Only after the nurse had put the catheter in correctly did the grimace that Ray had been working so hard to mask begin to disappear.

I actually got a little mad at him. "Why didn't you say something about it sooner?"

"I don't know. Guess I didn't want to bother anybody."

That, I explained to Ron, was Ray in a nutshell. "He can be real stoic when it comes to pain," I told him. "Even if they were beating him with a two-by-four, he wouldn't say anything. So you need to tell whoever's looking after him to make sure he gets stripped down to nothing and have them check every inch of his body for bruises and possible broken bones because, even if he's hurt, Ray's not going to tell you. He'd just suck it up because he'd much rather suffer than complain. That's just the kind of guy he is. He's stubborn as a mule."

"I can assure you that he'll be getting a very thorough physical exam. I doubt they would try to beat him, but if for some reason they did—trust me—we'd find out about it and quickly put a stop to it. I know this must be terribly stressful for you. How are you holding up?"

"Some media people showed up at my house today, which is a little annoying. They've set up shop right outside my house. They're practically camping in my front yard. Other than that, I can't complain. I'm sure everything's going to be all right."

"I can't tell you how relieved I am you're taking this so well. Most people in your shoes would be a nonstop fountain of tears."

"Not much use in doing that, is there? I just have to trust that everything's going to be fine. Ray's been trained to deal with situations like this. If anyone can handle it, it's him."

12.

LAHORE CANTONMENT, LAHORE, PAKISTAN
(January 28, 2011—Day 2)

I F I SLEPT AT ALL THAT FIRST NIGHT, it couldn't have been for more than fifteen or twenty minutes at a time. Still concerned about my safety after the guard who was left alone with me pulled out his gun, I made myself snap to attention every time someone moved, and with four guards in the room with me at all times that happened multiple times per hour. It didn't help that the overhead lights and the television in the corner stayed on the entire time. I'd had worse nights, plenty of them, but this one was right up there. It was a relief when dawn finally arrived.

The guards rousted me from bed, telling me I needed to get ready for court. They also said they were going to McDonald's and asked me what I wanted for breakfast. Only then did it hit me: I hadn't eaten anything since noon the day before.

While the guards were out getting me food, I was left alone in the room with the young lieutenant who'd caught me trying to delete data from my GPS and who seemed to be a lot sharper than his older comrades. As I sat there waiting, he smirked at me and nodded his head at the television. I looked up and saw footage from the scene of the incident playing on a local news channel. I saw the motorcycle the two men had been riding laying on its side. I saw the white sedan with some of its windows busted out. And I saw what seemed like a never-ending loop of angry crowds, some of them holding signs calling for my death. But the newscaster was speaking in Urdu, so I couldn't tell exactly what was being said.

"Those two men you shot yesterday?" said the young lieutenant. "They expired."

He waited for me to say something, but I chose not to.

"The man on the motorcycle who got hit by the SUV? He also expired."

The way I was staring at him, he might as well have been wallpaper.

"And now the wife of one of the men you shot? She swallowed some poison last night and killed herself."

This got my attention. Were they going to try to pin one more death that I had nothing to do with on me? But I just sat there, refusing to say a word.

The young lieutenant leaned closer to me. "All of these deaths are on your hands. You will be held accountable for them."

I think he just wanted to see what kind of reaction I would have. I didn't give him much. I continued to stare straight ahead, not saying a word. I tried to project a sense of confidence, but any sense I'd had that this matter might be resolved quickly and in my favor was beginning to erode.

I could only hope that my court appearance went well.

AS MANDATED BY PAKISTAN'S CODE of Criminal Procedure, the police had twenty-four hours from the time of the incident to document the "cognizable offence," which I'd allegedly committed, in a First Information Report (FIR) and to file the FIR with the magistrate, who would then determine whether there were grounds for a case. Roughly eighteen hours after the incident, I was led into a cramped courtroom by a police officer who'd placed one end of a Darby cuff—an old-fashioned and clunky handcuff once common in Britain—around my right wrist and the other end to himself. If I tried to run away, I'd have to drag him with me.

The courtroom was tiny and full of people. I looked around for the RSO or anyone else from the consulate, but I was disappointed to find that I was the only American in the room. The prosecutor, Asad Manzoor Butt, had a handful of aides assisting him, but not a single person was there to represent me. Thinking about being on trial in Pakistan without any legal representation or assistance from the consulate gave me a sick feeling in my stomach. While the US government ultimately picked up the tab for my services, at the end of the day I was a self-employed independent contractor responsible for my own well-being. There was a chance I could be on my own here, and I wasn't sure what to think about that.

After a few opening remarks, the prosecutor approached me. "From your statement it appears you don't deny killing those two men on Jail Road, correct?" he asked in English.

"That's right."

"How do you wish to plead?"

I looked over both of my shoulders, hoping someone from the consulate might suddenly appear, before giving the prosecutor a puzzled look. "Not guilty? Self-defense? I don't know what to say."

I began to feel a little more at ease when the judge took his seat and asked Officer Kazmi, the deputy superintendent of the district where the shooting had taken place, to provide an account of the incident. Kazmi's version was nearly identical to the one I'd given the day before. "Mr. Davis was in his car and the man on the back of the motorcycle drew a gun," he said, "and Mr. Davis responded by drawing his gun and shooting through the windshield at the men on the motorcycle."

I was encouraged that the police seemed to be doing their best to find the truth and from what I could tell seemed to be acting aboveboard. The same couldn't be said for the prosecutor, Butt, who interrupted Kazmi's narrative by whispering in the officer's ear. A quizzical look came over Kazmi's face, and when he resumed speaking it was entirely in Urdu. The only parts of his story I could understand were the ones he illustrated with his hands, like when he made a jabbing motion with his index finger to show how the shots I'd fired had burned holes through the sedan's windshield.

When Kazmi finished, the prosecutor turned to me and asked, "Do you speak our language? Do you speak Urdu?"

"No. No, I do not."

"I heard that you do. Someone told me you spoke Urdu."

I could only imagine that he thought this because I understood a few words like *pani* and *naswar*. Or he was simply doing what the Pakistani authorities had done to so many other Americans in the past few years and was trying to make me look like a spy.

The prosecutor turned to the judge and started talking to him in Urdu.

"I'm sorry, sir," I said to the judge. "I only speak English. I can't follow what you-all are saying."

The prosecutor and the judge spoke briefly in English before switching back to Urdu for good. This, I would later discover, was not uncommon.

Court proceedings in Pakistan are supposed to be conducted in English, but they tend to lapse into Urdu fairly quickly, particularly at informal hearings such as this one. This didn't make it any less confusing for me. Unable to follow what they were saying and lacking any legal representation, I had no idea what was going on. I would only find out later that the men I'd shot weren't exactly stand-up guys. Together they had been arrested more than fifty times and had police records as long as my arm. Even more incriminating: At the time of the incident they were carrying stolen cell phones, and neither of the guns they possessed was licensed.

And yet, despite all of that, the prosecutor, Butt, still tried to portray me as the bad guy, even going so far as to claim, falsely, that I'd stepped outside of my car and shot Haider in the back as he was running away. It was clear that this was going to be anything but an open-and-shut case. The judge ordered that I be held in jail for a fourteen-day "physical remand," while the police further investigated the shooting at Mozang Chowk.

This was my introduction to the Pakistani legal system. Remarkably, as strange as my first trip to court was, it wouldn't be the oddest of my ordeal. Not even close.

AFTER MY INITIAL COURT APPEARANCE, I was hustled into a vehicle that was waiting for me outside. In such an environment, where I had no idea what was going on from one minute to the next, I knew that gaining any new information, no matter how small, could end up being useful. Before we started driving, I looked at the odometer and made a mental note of the mileage, and 23.1 kilometers later, after driving south on Canal Road, we arrived at the Lahore Police Training College.

The fact that the police kept moving me from one location to the next concerned me, as it made the RSO's job—finding me and protecting me—that much more difficult. Even more disturbing, the place where they took me was like a fortress, with guards armed with AK-47s standing at nearly every corner. I was led into a very basic room where I was left to stew alone for several hours until a guard poked his head in and said, "Interview." I didn't know exactly what he meant by this, but I imagined the police wanted to question me some more. So it was a very pleasant surprise when the guard led me to a little cubicle inside a large room down the hall and directed me to sit on the other side of a table where a team from the US Consulate in Lahore was gathered.

The first person I recognized was Carmela Conroy. As consul general, she was in charge of the entire consulate in Lahore, answerable only to Ambassador Munter in Islamabad. I'd previously met her at the consulate, and had attended some social events at her house in Lahore. Her Thanksgiving and Christmas parties were especially well known. One time she even invited my team and various consulate personnel to her house to watch a samurai movie, which actually wasn't as random as it sounds. Before working in Lahore (and before that Afghanistan, where she was regional refugee coordinator), she was stationed in Okinawa and Tokyo, where she fell in love with Japanese culture.

A career diplomat, she seemed just as comfortable mingling with heads of state as she did chatting with a knuckle-dragger like me, which might explain how I was soon addressing her by her first name. Being able to communicate effectively with people from all sorts of different backgrounds and cultures was an important part of her job, and Carmela did it extremely well. She could bridge almost any gap, so I always felt comfortable in her presence, but never more so than now.

As I entered the room, she stood up from the table, offered me her hand, and studied me. "How are you holding up, Ray?"

"I'm doing all right."

A man stepped from behind her. "I'm Dale Rush. I'm the regional medical officer for the embassy." He lowered his voice to a whisper. "I'm also an 18 Delta."

An 18 Delta was a medical sergeant in SF. Thanks to the army's use of alphanumeric codes, Dale didn't have to come right out and say, "I'm an SF medic," which might have aroused some suspicion. All he had to say was, "I'm an 18 Delta," and I knew exactly what he was talking about. That I'd be able to communicate with him without anyone knowing what we were actually saying was a bit of a relief.

"Let me just take a quick look at you." The haphazard way Dale placed his stethoscope all over my chest made me think for a second that he wasn't actually a doctor. As he moved it from place to place, he asked, "So how are you doing?"

"I'm fine."

He leaned in closer to me and whispered, "No, really, how are you?"

I understood he was looking for more information, and I gave him what I could. "Well, the Pineland games haven't started yet, brother."

Pineland was the "fictional country" in the middle of North Carolina where I underwent SERE training as part of my SF Qualification Course. One of the focuses of the training was teaching us how to deal with incarceration and detention. We were treated as prisoners of war and subjected to various types of abuse and torture. For example, we were crammed inside very small containers called "dog boxes" for about a minute so we would know exactly how it felt. If you were claustrophobic, it must have been horrible. Otherwise, it wasn't so bad. Unless, of course, you were really big. Because of my size, I actually broke the box I was put in.

SERE wasn't a hands-off experience. It was very much hands-on. Basically, the instructors beat the crap out of us. During the three weeks I was there, they hit me so hard they dislocated my jaw, paralyzed a nerve in my neck, and severely damaged my right lung. It was this last injury that would later force me out of the army. With my reference to Pineland, I was telling Dale, without having to use the actual word, that I wasn't being tortured.

Dale nodded. "Okay, got it. But I'm still going to have to give you a physical exam. Can you take your shirt off?"

"Sure."

He examined my body with so much attention and focus I could have been a horse he was contemplating buying. He did everything but check my teeth to determine my age before pointing to a little bruise on my chest. His scrutiny of me seemed excessive, almost like something Rebecca would put me through after returning from a tour overseas.

"What's that?" he asked.

The bruise was so small I could barely see it. "I don't know."

"Are they hitting you?"

"No."

"Are you being honest with me?"

"Yes."

"All right then."

I went to put my shirt back on. "Are we done here?"

"Actually, I need you to take your pants off."

"Seriously? I'm fine. No one's touched me."

"I understand, but I was told I needed to check *everywhere*."

Carmela excused herself and stepped outside of the room. I took off my pants, and Dale did everything but make me cough. He was so thorough in his inspection of my lower half it irritated me a little.

"Are we good?"

"Yep, all done. Everything checks out. I just had to make sure."

Dale told Carmela she could come back in. She returned to her chair and, after assuring me that my wife and son were being taken care of, she handed me a notebook and pen. "If you'd like to write a note to your family, I'll make sure it gets to them. And if there's anything else I can do for you, anything at all, just let me know."

I took the notebook and pen from her. "I can't think of anything right now. I guess I'd just like to know what's going on and what exactly you-all are doing to get me out of here."

"We're working on it, Ray. I'm doing everything in my power. I promise you."

"That sounds good. I trust you-all to do your jobs. But time is moving quick. More than a day has passed already. And I know that if I don't get out of here soon I'm going to be in here for a while."

"No, you can't think like that. I promise you we're working on this as hard as we possibly can. We're going to get you released soon."

I nodded. "I appreciate all that you're doing. Really I do. But I know the statistics. In a situation like this, if you're not out in forty-eight hours, you need to be prepared for the *long* haul."

13.

LAS VEGAS, NEVADA
(February 2007)

W HEN I FIRST MET RAY, *he was very open with his feelings. For someone who looked so physically imposing, he was actually quite sensitive. I saw him cry more often than you would imagine. When we watched sappy movies together, he could be a regular fountain of tears! But as soon as Ray started contracting, he shut down emotionally. He also didn't share many details about his job. To be honest, I never really knew what Ray did. He was always very reserved when it came to discussing his work. He never talked about particular assignments or details of a mission. Ray was like a bank vault. Once valuable information got inside, it sat behind a very heavy, locked door, to be accessed only by those with a need to know.*

REBECCA KNEW WHAT I DID FOR A LIVING, but no one else did. When people asked me what kind of work I did, I told them I performed risk assessments on buildings. Being discreet was an essential part of my job. When you're assigned to protect people, one of the most dangerous things you can ever do is open your mouth. So I didn't. I never talked about what I did or what I saw or who I was protecting with anyone. Not even with my siblings or Rebecca's.

One day Rebecca's youngest sister was talking to Rebecca and me about her husband. "He's so stressed out," she said.

I snickered a little. "Really? What does he have to be stressed about? He's a commercial real estate broker."

"You wouldn't understand, Ray," Rebecca's sister said. "You just sit in an office and write reports all day. You wouldn't know what stress is."

I shrugged, because what else could I do? "Yeah, I guess you're right."

I'D BEEN RIGHT ABOUT RAY. Once he started contracting, he never wanted to stop. It seemed like he wasn't home five minutes from one deployment before he started talking about the next one. Sometimes he'd stay home three or four, sometimes even six months, depending on the contract, but a lot of times it would only be two or three weeks, and that was never enough time for him to fully decompress or for me to feel like I truly had a husband. Then before you knew it, we were getting ready to say good-bye again. Like so many others around the globe, our family was being held hostage by the War on Terror.

Whenever Ray left, it was awful. There were days I couldn't even get out of bed.

"Why don't you go somewhere?" he often suggested. "Take a cruise or something."

"With who?" I'd respond. "I don't have anybody to do stuff with. Everyone I know works and has kids."

If there's a lonelier life than being a military contractor's wife, I don't want to know what it is. I knew that Ray was just doing his job and that he couldn't earn anywhere close to the amount of money he was making doing anything else, and yet I still wanted him to quit and stay home. We were apart so often I jumped at any opportunity to see him, even if it meant driving from Las Vegas to Virginia in the middle of winter, as I once did. Right in the middle of the trip a huge snowstorm hit, and I was forced to hole up in a motel in Colby, Kansas, for a couple days. Once the storm finally passed, I immediately got back on the road because another storm was on its way and I didn't want to be stuck in Kansas a minute longer. Even after the first storm had cleared, it still took me six hours to get from Colby to Salina, which is usually no more than a three-hour drive. All this just to hang out with Ray for a couple days on the East Coast after he did some training at DynCorp's campus in Virginia.

Beyond the normal inclination of a wife who hasn't seen her husband in a while, I had further motivation for wanting to spend some quality time with Ray: He'd told me that for his next contract DynCorp was sending him to Iraq. He'd worked there the summer before, and when he'd returned he'd told me he'd never go back there again. It was that bad. News reports confirmed his apprehension. People were dying left and right over there. But at the same time he needed the work. Funny how the need to pay bills always wins out. He went ahead and signed the contract with DynCorp, leaving me to fret about it.

"I know if you go to Iraq, you're going to die," I told him. "I want to see you before you go."

I TOLD REBECCA I WAS GOING TO BE ON THE EAST COAST for a couple weeks in between deployments, and she drove all the way there from Las Vegas with our dog Remington just to hang out with me for a couple days before we drove home together. I was supposed to go to Iraq, and she was scared because that year was one of the deadliest of the entire war.

She got stuck in a blizzard in Kansas, and it took her forever to drive across country, but she finally made it. We met up in Reston, Virginia, during my last week of training and spent a few days together at Virginia Beach. That's when I told her that the plan had changed, that I wasn't going to Iraq anymore, that I was going to Afghanistan instead.

"That's such good news," she said, looking visibly relieved. "Everything's going to be fine now."

I GOT PREGNANT IN JANUARY 2008. Our son was born on September 29, and Ray was home from August 16 to December 26. That was a really nice time. For the first three months of our son's life, we were all together and I actually got some sleep. Ray and I would take shifts. I would get up at 3 or 4 A.M. to feed the baby and relieve Ray, and then Ray would sleep until 11 or 12. Then we would have the whole day together because I wouldn't go to bed until 10 or 11 at night. It worked out where we were both getting at least four to six hours of sleep when a lot of couples who have babies only get two or three here and there. I got more sleep those first three months than I ever did later on. It was a nice little routine while it lasted.

The best part was that we got to spend time together as a family. Ray was there not only for our son's birth, but also for our son's first Halloween, his first Thanksgiving, and his first Christmas. During Ray's entire contracting career, this was the only time he was home for Halloween and Thanksgiving and one of the few times he was home for Christmas. Then he left the day after Christmas, and it was back to the normal routine.

He wasn't home very much after that.

I DIDN'T MIND MISSING A BIT OF SLEEP while I was home during my son's first three months. It was an incredible time. Getting to see him and Rebecca every day, watching him grow, being together as a family—it was really nice.

Rebecca even taught me and our baby boy sign language. The very first day after we brought him home from the hospital, we started practicing. She taught us the signs for "milk" and "more" and "crackers" as well as many others. Some of our relatives thought we were a little goofy.

"What are you doing?" one of them asked. "He can barely even see yet."

"It's more for us right now," Rebecca explained.

IT'S FUNNY—PUT RAY IN A WAR ZONE, and he'll be just fine, but when I first handed him the baby, he was completely lost. He didn't know what to do with him. I imagine it's that way with a lot of new dads, but I was so tired I really didn't care. I just needed some relief. When our son was about six months old, I asked Ray to take care of him for a little while so I could take a nap, but Ray couldn't do it. He just couldn't do it. Five minutes after I'd handed him the baby, Ray walked into our bedroom.

"He misses you."

"Ray, please, I just need a little sleep."

"I don't know what to do with him."

"Sure you do."

"Nothing's making him happy. I think he just wants to be with you."

"For god's sake, Ray. Stick him in the buzzy chair, put on Baby Einstein, *and get yourself a beer. Or—I don't know—talk to him. It's not rocket science."*

It wasn't his fault. I just don't think Ray knew how to handle being a dad in the very beginning. Does anyone? You can't understand how hard it is until you go through it yourself. Only then do you really know. When Ray was home, he was great with our son. He changed his diapers. He fed him. He did his part. He was a good dad. No, he was a great *dad.*

But then, like clockwork, he'd leave, and whenever he left, he just kind of
fell off the radar.

AFTER WORKING IN HOSTILE ENVIRONMENTS for so many years, I
started to think I could handle just about anything. My Skill Jar was
filling up. I was on my way to becoming an Old Warrior. But I'll admit
there were times when Rebecca left me in charge of our son and I was
like, "What do I do?!"

There was this one time when my son was about fourteen months
old that I'll never forget. He was eating solid foods, but he wasn't talking
yet. Rebecca went to run some errands and left the two of us home alone
together. He started to get upset, so I put him in his high chair and gave
him some of the food Rebecca had left out for him and a sippy cup full
of milk, but he didn't want any of it. He pushed the cup away and threw
some of the food on the floor, and he was crying the whole time.

I felt so helpless. "What is it? I don't understand. What do you want?"

He pointed to the cabinet and made the sign for crackers.

I almost didn't believe it at first. Was he really asking me for crackers?
I grabbed a handful from the cabinet and set them down in front of him,
and he stopped crying and started eating them.

No exaggeration—it was one of the most amazing things I'd ever
seen. He was communicating with me! He was telling me exactly what
he wanted! It blew me away. All that training Rebecca had done with
him was now paying off.

As soon as he was done with the crackers, he pointed to the refrigerator.

"What is it? What do you want?"

He made the sign for cheese.

"Okay! Cheese. Let me get some for you."

I gave him some cheese, and then he made the sign for juice.

"Oh, now I get it. You don't want milk. You want juice."

I got him some juice. He was happy. *We* were happy. It was incredible.

OUR SON WAS BORN WITH ALL SORTS OF MEDICAL PROBLEMS. When he
was a baby, he would only drink eight to ten ounces of formula a day. He had

acid reflux, sleep apnea, night terrors, and something called hydronephrosis, which is swelling of a kidney due to the normal flow of urine being obstructed. It was just one thing after another as far as his health and sleep went.

But none of his doctors would listen to me. I knew something was wrong with him, but it was like they didn't trust what I was telling them was true. I told them he wasn't eating, but they didn't believe it until he spent a week in the hospital when he was four months old, and none of the nurses or doctors could get him to eat.

A month later, a growth appeared in my son's groin. The doctors told me it was normal. I stared at them in disbelief and pointed at my son's upper thigh. "You're telling me that huge *lump is normal?" We got bounced around from one doctor to the next. One would say it was okay, another would say it wasn't okay. I trusted the one who said it wasn't okay. He said my son had a renal hernia and should have surgery right away, so that's what we did.*

I had to take my son to the pediatrician once a week and to a specialist two or three times a week, and all of the pediatricians we went to were so condescending and mean and hateful. I switched doctors eight times before my son even had his first birthday. This one doctor was the worst. *I took my son to her because he was having trouble breathing, and she actually told me that all babies breathe funny. I had a meltdown right there in her office. I started screaming, "Somebody please help my baby! He's not breathing right! Something's not right! I need help!" When she continued to insist that he was fine, I took him to an ear, nose, and throat specialist, who told me our son's adenoids were swollen and his nasal passages were blocked as much as 80 to 90 percent!*

Surgery fixed that problem, but then it was on to the next one. Our son had an appendectomy when he was seven months old. He had his tonsils taken out when he was two years and three months old. And in between all the trips to the hospital he was always getting sick. He got all these weird illnesses, like respiratory syncytial virus. And I had to do all these emergency trips to the hospital, every doctor's visit, everything, *all by myself. Ray was gone the entire time, so I had no one there to help me. No emotional support, no pats on the back,* nothing. *And my anxiety was going through the roof. I was terrified. What if my son suddenly stopped breathing in the middle of the night? What if he never started to put on weight? Was he ever going to get better? After what they put me through, I hated taking my son to the doctor, but I had no choice. We practically* lived *at the doctor's office.*

I was filled with so much anxiety I was barely sleeping. I'd get a couple hours here, a couple hours there. It was awful. The fact that Ray was gone all the time didn't help, and when he was there it was almost more aggravating because he wasn't worth a darn. He would never have admitted it, but after what he experienced overseas, he just wasn't able to cope when he came home. So I was never able to get a break or get caught up on sleep. I was so sleep-deprived I don't remember a lot of the details. It's a blur.

I would never want to go back to that time.

I WAS GONE MUCH MORE THAN I WAS HOME. That was just the nature of my occupation. Being away from home so much was tough, but I knew Rebecca had the harder job. When I was gone, she had to deal with our son being sick all the time, and she had to do it all by herself. My job might have been more dangerous, but hers was definitely more difficult.

Before our son was even born, the doctor told us he had hydronephrosis. I freaked out in the elevator as we were leaving the hospital. There was another doctor in there with us, and he asked what was wrong, and I told him, and he said not to worry. "The machines we're using now have gotten so advanced we can detect things that will never become problematic," he said. "Your son may very well grow out of it, and if he does end up needing surgery, it's a real simple fix."

BEYOND THE EMOTIONAL TOLL OUR SON'S health issues took on us, they were expensive. Normal baby-related expenses are bad enough. Diapers, wipes, and formula add up quickly. But when you throw in all the doctor's visits and surgeries and prescriptions we had to pay for, it was out of control. We were spending $2,000 a month on our son. I don't know how people do it. I figured out a way to get his Nexium prescription reduced from $200 a month to $25 and the special formula he had to take, which cost $600 a month, for free, but if Ray had been making any less I don't know how we would have managed.

Looking for a way to reduce our household's expenses, we decided to start our own business: Hyperion Protective Services. Ray continued to do the same security contract work he'd done before, contracting directly with the US government. Doing this had almost no discernible impact on the way he did his job, but come tax time, the impact was huge. Previously, Ray would get 1099s and we'd have to pay a ton of taxes; now because we owned our own company and worked for ourselves we didn't have to pay quite so much.

Starting our own company had another great advantage. We'd had a difficult time getting even halfway decent health insurance in the past because Ray and I were both injured in the army, but now we were eligible for a small-group health insurance plan that provided excellent coverage, which meant our son would always be covered. We considered this a huge benefit at the time, but its full value wasn't felt until we found out several years later that our son's kidney problem was more severe than the doctors had originally thought. He was going to need surgery once again.

WHEN I WAS IN SF, the most I ever made was $34,000 a year. That was my base pay. On top of that, I got $150 each month I jumped out of a plane. This was called Hazardous Duty Incentive Pay. It never added up to very much, but, of course, I didn't do the job to get rich. I did it to serve and protect my country.

The most I ever earned as a contractor was $172,000 a year. People tend to make a big deal about how much contractors make, but they're only looking at one number. They don't realize that while we're working we're on call 24/7, so our effective hourly rate isn't nearly as great as it first appears. They also tend to forget that a big portion of our income goes to paying taxes (whereas those members of the Armed Forces serving in a war zone don't have to pay taxes, thanks to combat zone tax exclusions). Another big chunk gets eaten up paying for health insurance. I also had to pay for all my own gear, including, but not limited to, web utility vests, hydration systems, medical supplies, holsters, and the all-important and incredibly expensive Kevlar and ceramic-plate body armor.

The army also takes care of you and your family when you retire or die. Veterans receive a pension, and close relatives of those killed in combat get death benefits. For contractors, it's a much different story. Once you sign the overly detailed and generally one-sided contract with a private military-contracting company, you're pretty much on your own. There is no retirement fund, and the best your family can hope for if you get killed is to take advantage of insurance provided by the Defense Base Act, which covers some, but not all, contractors supporting US military operations and which pays, at most, $65,000.

As much as I liked the job, I was always aware of how I fit in the grand scheme of things. Contractors are basically the plastic cutlery of the military: extremely useful and cost-effective but ultimately disposable.

Working as a military contractor in Afghanistan in 2005

Rebecca and I on our honeymoon in the Florida Keys in March 2004

Rebecca and I on vacation in Istanbul, Turkey, in October 2004

In 2005, several years after rehabbing my lung riding a bike, I completed the 100-mile El Tour de Tucson bike ride

Playing football my senior year at Powell Valley High School in Big Stone Gap, Virginia

Rebecca at Fort Bragg, North Carolina, in 1998 when she was a member of the 82nd Airborne

A shot of me in Tucson, Arizona, after (finally!) graduating from college (American Military University) in May 2005

"Lawyer's Lane" in Lahore, where a large percentage of local attorneys have offices, including my lawyer Zahid Hussein Bukhari (© Peter Strasser)

A typical sight in Lahore, where people are known to carry everything but the kitchen sink on their motorcycles (© Peter Strasser)

The staff of the US Consulate in Lahore, Pakistan (2009). Seated front row left to right: Special Representative for Afghanistan and Pakistan Richard Holbrooke, Consul General Carmela Conroy, Secretary of State Hillary R. Clinton, and Ambassador Anne Patterson (© Ali Agha)

Hillary R. Clinton and Carmela Conroy unveil the new consulate general seal at a ceremony held at the US Consulate General in Lahore (2009) (© Ali Agha)

Celebrating Easter with my son in Las Vegas, Nevada, in April 2011

14.

LAHORE POLICE TRAINING COLLEGE, LAHORE, PAKISTAN
(January 29, 2011—Day 3)

O NE OF THE HARDEST ASPECTS of my incarceration was that, at least in the beginning, I had no way of knowing how long it might last. As helpful as the consulate personnel had been during their initial visit, they hadn't been able to give me a definitive date when I might be released, leading me to believe that I was going to be held for a very long time. Did that mean a week, a month, a year—*multiple* years? I didn't know, and I wasn't prepared to think that far ahead. All I could do was take it one day at a time, sometimes just one hour at a time, and hope that my next day there would be my last, while also not allowing myself to get overly disappointed when it wasn't.

When you're being held against your will in a foreign country, your mind can get the better of you, convincing you of the hopelessness of your situation. Fortunately, I'd been trained how to deal with this sort of doomsday thinking before it could spiral out of control. I knew it was important for me to ignore negative thoughts about the future in favor of positive ones about the present. What could I do *right now* to better my plight?

One thing I could do was sleep. If my captors were going to start depriving me of sleep, a subtle but effective form of torture, the best way for me to combat this would be to sleep as much as possible before it started. With that in mind, as soon as the consulate personnel left, I crawled into bed, pulled a blanket over myself, and somehow managed to sleep for twenty-two hours straight! I might have made it to a full twenty-four, but a guard woke me to tell me that the team from the consulate had returned for another meeting.

Using the notebook and pen Carmela had given me during our first meeting, I'd written a note to Rebecca and my son, telling them how much I loved them and missed them and assuring them that everything was going to be fine (even though I wasn't entirely sure that was true). When Carmela stood to greet me after I walked into the same room where we'd met the previous day, I made a big show of handing her the note and asking her to see that it got delivered to my wife and son. She assured me that she would. I didn't care if the guards read this note or even confiscated it. Everything I wrote in it my family already knew. But I really didn't want them to find the other note I'd written and hidden in the watch pocket of my jeans.

Thanks to the relatively kind way I'd been treated so far, I was fairly certain that my captors were unaware of which branch of the military I'd served in, what sort of training I'd had, or why I was in Pakistan. Rebecca and I had started our own security company in 2008, with me doing the actual contract work and her keeping the books. Doing it this way allowed us to cut out the middleman; instead of being employed by a private company, I worked for myself and contracted directly with the US government.

I was enlisted to protect State Department personnel. Did this make me a diplomat? Of course not. But for a country with Pakistan's paranoid tendencies—a conspiracy theory hadn't been dreamed up that was too implausible for its citizens to believe—any affiliation I might have had with another agency could be damning. If the police had thought this, I imagine they would have treated me with much less benevolence. I had no intention of assisting them. The second note I'd written said something to the effect of, "Please keep my special forces background quiet. Do not let them know who I am or where I come from. They're trying to paint me as a spy!"

I handed this note to Carmela's assistant Shane, shoving it into his palm as I was shaking his hand. I made sure he felt it before removing my hand. He acted a little surprised and for a second I thought he might actually say something about it, but then he closed his hand around the note and casually shoved his fist into one of the pockets of his jacket.

Shane wasn't a very big guy, but he had a big personality. He was very vocal, theatrical, and funny, and it appeared that he and Carmela had worked out a routine that took advantage of his natural enthusiasm because from time to time Shane would start talking even louder than usual, and whenever he did Carmela would lean closer to me and whisper so the guards in the room couldn't hear.

"Are they treating you all right?" she asked on one of these occasions.

"As well as can be expected."

"I'm not going to lie to you, Ray. Getting you out of here has proved to be much more difficult than we first thought. They're insisting that you be held for questioning. We're working on getting you a lawyer. In the meantime, you don't have to tell them anything if you don't want to. If they press you, all you have to say is that you're a diplomat accredited to the US Embassy and that you demand to be turned over to the diplomatic mission in Islamabad. Got it?"

I nodded and thanked her for all that she was doing.

"They can only hold you for fourteen days," she continued. "It's called physical remand. During this time, the police can question you as much as they want while they try to build a case against you." She got up to leave. "I can't say it's going to be easy, but you just need to keep reminding yourself that after fourteen days they can't question you anymore. Think you can handle it?"

The idea that I might not be able to make it through fourteen days of questioning almost made me laugh. Carmela obviously didn't know how much and what sort of training I'd done. I smiled as much for her sake as mine. "Shoot, that's nothing. I can last fourteen days. You don't have to worry about me. Fourteen days is easy!"

FOR THOSE WHO ENJOY watching TV shows like *Dual Survival* and *Man vs. Wild*, the SERE course I took as part of the SF Qualification Course might not seem like such a big deal. But let me tell you—there's a big difference between watching someone eat a snake or drink his own urine and having to do it yourself.

I'm a big guy. I like to eat. So it was a huge shock to my system when, for the better part of the three-week course, I was told I could eat only what I could find. No food was provided for us. We had to make do with whatever we could scavenge from the land. If we found some nuts or berries, we were lucky. Otherwise, we subsisted on grass, leaves, and bugs.

Rumor had it that one team actually found a deer that had been hit by a car, and they pulled it out of the road and ate strips of meat off of it until there was nothing left but bones and hooves. My team was at the opposite end of Pineland, so we never got to eat any venison. For all I know, the story about the deer might have been some cruel joke, one more way of messing with our minds.

During one stretch of my SERE training, I didn't eat anything for four or five days. For the next four or five days after that, it got a little better but not by much. Once a day we were given half a cupful of rice with some sardines mashed into it. It was enough to keep you alive, but that was about it. We were hungry all the time. As difficult as it was, the hunger we carried around with us each day brought with it one benefit: It kept us alert, sharp, and focused.

Remembering that experience and hoping to gain control over at least one aspect of my existence while being detained, I started refusing to eat everything I was given. After picking up food for me from McDonald's and Pizza Hut the first couple of days, the guards started giving me chicken curry and rice, which might sound pretty good until you consider that I only got two meals a day and both of them were *always* chicken curry and rice. They actually gave me a fairly large quantity, too—about six ounces of chicken and nearly two pounds of rice were fairly typical—but I purposely declined to eat it all.

You know how a newborn puppy latches onto one of his mother's teats and just drinks and drinks and drinks, and then all of a sudden he's completely out of it and falls asleep, and you can't wake him up? I call that "puppy tummy," and I didn't want the same thing happening to me. I wanted to stay as clearheaded as I could, so I'd make myself stop eating before I ever got full.

I also made a point of staying hydrated. The guards would give me a one-liter bottle of water, and I would drink it all within an hour or two, then hand the empty bottle back to them and ask for more. Tired of fetching a new bottle for me every couple of hours, they brought in several boxes full of bottled water and allowed me to help myself. These boxes ended up serving a dual purpose. I would also use them to get a workout, repeatedly lifting them over my head or holding a box on each shoulder while doing squats.

Despite my best efforts, the police still controlled nearly every aspect of my existence. They confiscated my watch and phone early on, so I never had any idea what time it was. Adding to my confusion, they left the overhead lights on in my room 24/7. They also entered my room whenever they wanted, and with only fourteen days to build their case against me, their visits to question me were frequent.

Given what I knew about the Pakistani police, I wasn't expecting them to be very adept at getting information from me. They simply didn't have the manpower or the expertise to do the job right. There were only a dozen police investigators in Lahore, and each of them was responsible for nearly 250 cases every month. Some of the officers who questioned me were actually pretty good at it, but just as many were really bad, like the one who kept cutting me off.

"Are you doing okay, sir?" he asked me.

"Yes, I'm f—"

"Do you need any more water?"

"No, I've got—"

"And you're getting enough food?"

"Yes, I—"

He placed a chair next to the bed where I was reading a magazine and sat down. "Now about the shooting. We're hearing very different stories. I'd like to hear your side of the story again."

I put down my magazine. "You know, if you're looking to get any information out of me, you should at least let me finish answering one question before you start asking the next one. You really need to work on building a rapport with the person you're interrogating before you start questioning them." I went back to reading my magazine before leaving him with one final thought. "And, no, I'm not answering any more of your questions."

From the way he stalked out of the room, you would have thought I'd spit on him or something.

The way another officer attempted to question me just left me confused.

"How are you doing today, sir?" Officer Tariq asked.

He was a well-mannered, likable guy who spoke very good English, so I was happy to make small talk with him. "Fine."

"How are things going with your case?"

"Honestly, I don't know. I don't have an attorney yet."

His eyes got big. "This is not good. Not good at all. Everyone deserves an attorney. *Everyone.*"

"Well, obviously, not everyone. It doesn't seem like I'm going to be getting one anytime soon."

"Your embassy should get you one."

"I'm sure they're working on it."

Officer Tariq went on to tell me that his brother owned a used car lot in Atlanta, Georgia. When he started talking about all the people he knew in America, I thought I saw the angle he was playing. I assumed he was just building a rapport with me and would soon start asking me about the incident, but he never did. He never asked me what I was doing in Lahore or anything like that. He just wanted to talk about American movies and culture and what life in the United States was really like.

If Officer Tariq was actually trying to interrogate me, he had a very roundabout way of doing it. Far more direct was the officer who walked into my room, sat down, and said, "I have been trained by your FBI interrogation team." Not only was his approach different, so was his dress. While the other officers wore uniforms that clearly identified them as the police, this guy, in his white dress shirt, black tie, and sweater vest, looked more like a banker. He intrigued me so much I actually looked forward to seeing how he was going to try to extract information from me.

It quickly became apparent that he believed in going slow. For the first ten or twenty minutes, he didn't say a word, just sat there while I read my magazine. When he finally started asking me questions, they were completely innocuous:

"How are you?"

"Are you being treated well here so far?"

"Is there anything you need?"

"What do you think about Pakistan?"

I answered all his questions fairly matter-of-factly except for the last one. "That's a pretty broad question," I said. "What do you mean?"

"In general, do you think this is a good country?"

"Yeah, sure. You've got some decent people here."

"What do you know about Lahore?"

"Not much. I've only been here six days."

"Have you ever been to DHA?"

DHA, or Defense Housing Authority, was a planned community built for army officers in the 1970s and since converted to a high-end neighborhood full of Western amenities like fast-food restaurants, bookstores, and DVD rental shops. I'd driven through that area many times. But I wasn't about to admit to ever being in a specific location in Lahore. Our conversation was being recorded, and I knew that if I said, "Yeah, sure, I've been there. It's a nice place," the police might try to use that against me in court, claiming I'd confessed to being there when something bad happened. Because I knew they might try to use anything I said against me, I was extremely careful whenever I opened my mouth.

"No, what's that?"

"You don't know what DHA is?"

"No, I've got no idea what you're talking about."

"Okay, fine. Let's talk about the shooting."

"No, I'm sorry. I already told you-all everything I know about it. You have my written statement. I'm not answering any more questions about it."

He backed off, but continued to sit there for the rest of the day. He must have been in my room for at least six hours. He watched me eat lunch and dinner. He watched me while I did a workout. He even watched me go to the bathroom. Every once in a while he would try to sneak in a question about the incident, but I quickly shut him down every time. We went back and forth like that all day until finally, defeated, he got up and left.

15.

LAHORE POLICE TRAINING COLLEGE, LAHORE, PAKISTAN
(February 1, 2011—Day 6)

WHEN I WASN'T BEING QUESTIONED by the police, I was being shuttled back and forth to different courts. I went to one court for carrying an unlicensed weapon, another for shooting the two men at Mozang Chowk, and both of the courtrooms looked about the same: small, dark, and poorly ventilated. They resembled shoeboxes more than they did actual courts of law. One was no bigger than a couple hundred square feet. The other was actually closer to a hundred, and yet somehow dozens of people still managed to cram themselves inside it. In some ways, the cramped quarters reminded me of being inside a C-130 Hercules aircraft packed full of soldiers preparing to make a jump. Given the choice, I would have much rather been inside one of those planes.

On the days I was scheduled to appear in court, my routine generally remained the same. I would get up, shave, put on the suit the consulate personnel had brought me, and take whatever transportation was provided for me to the courthouse. The only thing that ever really changed was the prosecution's story.

The first time I went to court, the prosecutor, Butt, told the judge, "Your honor, Mr. Davis shot two armed men who tried to shoot him. Both of them had guns and ammunition."

The next time I went to court, Butt said, "Your honor, Mr. Davis shot two armed men, but they meant him no harm. Both of them were carrying guns, it's true, but they didn't have ammunition in the chamber, only in the magazine. Those men did not intend to hurt him." This erroneous account was backed up by Officer Tareen, who also claimed that I'd stepped out of the car and shot Faizan Haider as he was running away.

The third time I went to court, Butt claimed that the two men I'd shot were ISI agents. He told an elaborate story about them following me from some secret meeting in DHA that had gone bad. At the mention of DHA, I blanched, realizing just how close I'd come to being set up. If I'd admitted to the well-dressed officer who claimed he'd been trained by the FBI that I'd ever been to DHA, I promise you the prosecutor would have found a way to use that information against me.

The fourth time I went to court, Butt claimed that the two men on the motorcycle didn't even have guns. As frustrating as it was to hear such a brazen lie, it was even more frustrating that I couldn't disprove it. The police had taken my camera away from me (and therefore also the three photographs I'd taken of Muhammad Faheem that showed him holding a gun in his hand) the day of the incident.

That's how much the prosecutor's story changed from the first time I went to court to the fourth time. What bothered me the most was that the judge never intervened and said, "Wait a minute, you've given me four different versions of the event. Why do these stories vary so much? Which one is true? If one of them is true, the others must be false. Why are you fabricating information?"

As shocked as I was by Butt's lies and the judge's ineptitude, from what I'd read about the Pakistani legal system, I shouldn't have been. To bluntly summarize the 2008 USAID report *Pakistan Rule of Law Assessment*, the court system in Pakistan is a junk show. Judges are poorly paid, frequently threatened by terrorists, and expected to handle an impossible workload. Thanks to a system that encourages lawyers to use delaying tactics and doesn't allow plea bargaining, the courts suffer from an extremely high backlog of cases. Worse, when defendants finally do make it in front of a judge, they're often met with corruption. According to a 2010 State Department report, even Pakistan's Anti-Terrorism Courts, a parallel judicial system created by Prime Minister Nawaz Sharif in 1997 to expedite justice for those brought up on terrorism charges, had a shockingly high acquittal rate. Because of the ineptitude of bumbling prosecutors and intimidated judges, three out of every four suspected terrorists in Pakistan were found not guilty and let go.

As unfamiliar as the Pakistani legal system was to me, when combined with my inability to speak or understand Urdu and my lack of legal representation, it came to seem downright menacing. Before my fifth visit to court, I expressed my frustration to Carmela.

"Any chance someone will be there to represent me?"

"We're working on it," she said in such a way that made it clear she was every bit as annoyed as I was.

Heading into court that fifth time, I held out hope, as I always did, that a lawyer would be there to represent me, but when I stepped into the courtroom I didn't see a single American. I was greeted by the usual throng of Pakistani faces, and I resigned myself to the idea that I was going to have to represent myself once again.

Butt spoke first, and as soon as he finished the judge said, "All right, who here's from the defense?"

I was about to explain that I would be representing myself when a man emerged from the crowd and approached the judge's bench. He looked Pakistani, but when he opened his mouth and spoke it was clear that he was as American as a cooler full of Budweiser on the Fourth of July.

"I'm from the US Consulate, and I'll be speaking on behalf of Mr. Davis."

Samir wasn't a lawyer, but I was delighted to see him nevertheless. He spoke Urdu just as well as he spoke English, so, at the very least, he was able to explain to me exactly how I was being screwed.

"They want you to come back here Friday," he told me as soon as he was done talking to the judge. "Until then, you're just going to have to sit tight, okay?"

REGARDLESS OF WHETHER the men I'd shot had guns, the real issue, it quickly became apparent, was whether I had diplomatic immunity or not. The diplomatic passport and visa I'd used on previous trips to Pakistan had expired at the end of 2010. Prior to my return in January 2011, I'd been issued a new diplomatic passport, which was valid until 2016, as well as a new visa, which was valid until June 2012. Getting a visa had been just as easy as it had always been. For a US government official or contractor to get a visa into Pakistan, the request only had to be approved

by Pakistan's ambassador to the United States, Husain Haqqani, who had
lived in the United States since 2002 and was generally viewed as being
pro-American. Encouraged by the Pakistani government in Islamabad to
take a relaxed stance when granting visas to American officials, Haqqani
had approved mine and countless others.

The State Department had also notified the Pakistani government of
my assignment as far back as January 2010. The Pakistanis had responded
by asking the State Department to clarify my role. When the State Department failed to do so—evidently, this was part of the "sloppy recordkeeping" to which Ambassador Munter was referring—Pakistan's Ministry
of Foreign Affairs refused to issue me a diplomatic accreditation card,
citing the "unresolved queries" his office had made about me. Without
this essential document, which defines one's exact role at an embassy or
consulate, my status remained unclear.

In the days immediately following the incident in Lahore, the US
Embassy in Islamabad added to the confusion surrounding my status by
releasing a series of contradictory press releases. On January 28, it identified me as "a staff member of the US Consulate General in Lahore." The
following day, it referred to me as a "diplomat, assigned to the US Embassy
in Islamabad." And on January 30, it described me as "a member of the US
Embassy's technical and administrative staff." Despite good intentions,
these press releases only highlighted the lack of clarity about my status
and opened the subject up to debate.

Pakistani officials, angered by the growing presence of unidentified US officials in their country, pounced on the opportunity to use
my predicament to embarrass the United States and further their own
agendas. One of the most opportunistic was Shah Mahmood Qureshi,
the Cambridge-educated foreign minister who resigned from his post
on January 30 after being pressured by the central government to grant
me diplomatic immunity. Buoyed by his legal advisers, Qureshi seized
upon the fact that I worked for the consulate and not the embassy, and
he wouldn't let go. He said that after studying the Vienna Conventions
of 1961 and 1963, he had concluded that "the blanket immunity as being
demanded by the US Embassy was not valid."

According to the 1961 Vienna Convention on Diplomatic Relations,
"a diplomatic agent shall enjoy immunity from the criminal jurisdiction
of the receiving State," as should "members of the administrative and

technical staff of the mission." This was the focus of the counterargument the State Department put forth.

The sort of unmitigated immunity given to those who work in an embassy, however, isn't shared by those who work in a consulate. According to the 1963 Vienna Convention on Consular Relations, consular officers are granted immunity only from jurisdiction "in respect of acts performed in the exercise of consular functions."

This meant that until the Pakistanis could determine exactly where I worked and exactly what I did, they would continue to keep me in custody.

ON FEBRUARY 1, a bipartisan congressional delegation led by Representative Darrell Issa (R–California) met with Pakistan's President Asif Zardari and Prime Minister Yousaf Raza Gilani in separate meetings, asking them to honor the Vienna Convention on Diplomatic Relations and release me. Zardari had a very tenuous hold on his position; some attributed his rise to power not to his own political genius but to that of his wife, Benazir Bhutto, who had served two terms as prime minster before being assassinated in 2007.

Despite his good relations with the United States, Zardari simply wasn't strong enough politically to resolve my situation on his own. If he'd advocated for my release, it might have led to a national uprising and his removal from office. It didn't help that the incident had taken place right in the middle of the "Arab Spring."

On December 17, 2010, Tarek al-Tayeb Mohamed Bouazizi, a Tunisian street vendor protesting the confiscation of his vegetable cart and the daily constraints imposed by an oppressive government, had set himself on fire in front of a government office building in Tunis. His self-immolation set off a wave of antitotalitarian protests in the Middle East. Just two weeks before the incident in Lahore, the president of Tunisia, Zine el-Abidine Ben Ali, had resigned and fled to Saudi Arabia after weeks of mass protests demanding an end to his dictatorial regime.

The desire to see tyranny replaced with democracy quickly spread to Egypt, where, just two days before the incident at Mozang Chowk, Egyptian President Hosni Mubarak, in a sign of desperation as thousands of people took to the streets in protest, dismissed his government. Two weeks later, he, too, would be forced to step down.

One of the main factors that sparked the revolution in Egypt—a young population forced to deal with a high rate of unemployment and largely corrupt leaders—also existed in Pakistan. It didn't help that the incident I'd been involved in had taken place in Punjab Province, where Nawaz Sharif, the "Lion of the Punjab," ran a well-oiled political machine. Sharif had been prime minister from 1990 to 1993 and from 1997 to 1999, and as the leader of the Pakistan Muslim League, the country's largest political party and the chief opposition to President Zardari's regime, he had his sights set on an unprecedented third term in office. As prominent as Sharif was in the Punjab capital of Lahore, he greatly diminished Zardari's influence there. In the end, Zardari was happy to let others decide my fate. "It would be prudent to wait for the legal course to be completed," he said.

Like Zardari, who'd spent eleven years in jail over the course of his life (for corruption and murder), Prime Minister Gilani had spent five and a half years in jail (for corruption). Also like Zardari, Gilani wanted nothing to do with the growing diplomatic crisis the shooting at Mozang Chowk had ignited. Two days after Zardari had issued his statement about my case, Gilani said much the same on the floor of the National Assembly, the lower house of Pakistan's Parliament. Having pronounced the matter *sub judice*, or under consideration by a court and therefore protected from public debate, the two nominal leaders of Pakistan's government had refused to take a stance on the issue, passing it on to the Pakistani judicial system.

A lawyer filed a petition in the Lahore High Court that blocked any attempt to release me, and Chief Justice Ijaz Ahmed Chaudhry agreed. "I am restraining him [from being handed over to US authorities]. Whether he has or does not have [diplomatic] immunity will be decided by the court," he ruled.

Chaudhry backed up his words with action, putting my name on the country's Exit Control List. Created during a time of military rule in 1981, the list allowed the Pakistani government to prohibit anyone accused of a major offense within its borders, including drug traffickers, terrorists, and disgraced politicians, from leaving the country. This resulted in my name and photograph being sent to every airport, bus station, and border crossing in Pakistan.

The hole I'd been dragged into now had a heavy lid on it.

16.

LAHORE POLICE TRAINING COLLEGE, LAHORE, PAKISTAN
(February 6, 2011—Day 11)

I T WAS SOMETHING OF AN open secret that the Pakistani government used the media to create and shape stories they wished to see spread. My situation offered them the perfect opportunity to publicly rail against everything that bothered them about the increasingly heavy American presence in their country. The Pakistani government fed the media information that was speculative, salacious, and oftentimes untrue, and the Pakistani newspapers and television stations rarely shied away from running the stories. Many of these reports claimed I was a spy, others that I was an assassin. Failing to catch the redundancy, the *Nation*, an English newspaper in Lahore, described me as an "American Rambo."

The media didn't stop there. For whatever reason, Pakistanis love conspiracy theories. Pakistani journalist Mehdi Hasan once asked former cricket-star-turned-politician Imran Khan why. "They're lied to all the time by their leaders," he explained. "If a society is used to listening to lies all the time . . . everything becomes a conspiracy."

When former Pakistani president General Muhammad Zia-ul-Haq died in a mysterious plane crash on August 17, 1988, all sorts of conspiracy theories arose to explain it, including speculation that the CIA had orchestrated the crash (even though US Ambassador to Pakistan Arnold Raphel also died in the crash) or that India—of course!—was somehow involved. Another conspiracy theory commonly embraced in Pakistan was that Osama bin Laden was actually Jewish, while a similarly bizarre one suggested he was a US agent who'd died sometime in the mid-2000s.

So I really shouldn't have been all that surprised when I was told I'd become the subject of numerous conspiracy theories myself, many of which found their way into the Pakistani media and were treated as fact. They printed all kinds of crazy stories about me. They said that I was part of a Blackwater team who'd come to steal Pakistan's nuclear warheads and take over the country. They said I had pallets of liquor and hookers delivered to my cell each day. They said I had access to a cell phone and that I frequently talked to President Obama. They said I howled in my cell like some sort of crazy person whenever the call to prayer rang out. They said I was addicted to *naswar*. They even said I'd used "bone-melting bullets"—whatever that meant—that had been banned since 1898!

One of the most persistent—yet still untrue—conspiracy theories the Pakistani media spread about me was that I'd taken pictures of "sensitive areas," such as military forts and nuclear facilities. The photographs I'd actually taken were just silly, tourist-type shots of quintessentially Pakistani activities, the type of stuff you just don't see in America. One of seven people riding a motorcycle, for instance. Or a man walking a snake with a leash around its neck. Things I could tell you about, but you wouldn't believe unless you actually saw a picture of them.

Punjab law minister Rana Sanaullah tried to use the photographs allegedly found in my camera as evidence against me, portraying them as the handiwork of a spy. "This is not the work of a diplomat," he said. "He was doing espionage and other activities."

The most damning lie fabricated by the Pakistani government and disseminated by the media occurred toward the end of my fourteen-day physical remand, when the police were allowed to question me as much as they wanted. I heard about it from the consulate personnel during one of their visits. According to them, it was all over the news. Shumaila Kanwal, Muhammad Faheem's widow, had swallowed a lethal dose of poison and been rushed to Allied Hospital in Faisalabad. While lying on her deathbed, a television camera was thrust in her face, and she spoke about why she'd done it. "I do not expect any justice from this government," she said. "That is why I want to kill myself."

The media reported that she died a little before midnight. They also made her look like a martyr, releasing little details meant to tug at your heartstrings. Her mother was disabled. She had only been married to

Muhammad Faheem for six months. After he was killed, she became severely depressed.

What baffled and disturbed me was that I'd heard about her suicide *nine days* before it came out in the press. The young lieutenant at Lahore Cantonment had told me about it the morning after the incident had taken place. I can only speculate as to why the story remained hidden for so long. My best guess is that ISI forced the media to sit on it until it was needed to incite anti-American sentiment. Releasing the news the day after the incident when people were already protesting in the streets would have been redundant. But with the clock winding down on my physical remand and with the police having failed to get me to confess to a crime, this must have seemed like a good time to rile up the masses and apply some pressure on the government. If that was in fact the Pakistani government's plan, it worked. Activists from the socially conservative political party *Jamaat-e-Islami* gathered to protest outside the hospital where Kanwal allegedly died. Others demonstrated outside the consulate in Lahore.

The upshot of all this propaganda was that it turned me into a bogeyman in Pakistan, a monster people told their kids about before tucking them into bed. I'd come to represent all the fears and hatred against America that had been building up in Pakistan over time. The incident and the way it was being handled by the politicians, the courts, and the press had worked the people into a frenzy. They were protesting in the streets, burning effigies of me, and calling for me to be hanged. They carried posters of me with a noose around my neck and hung banners that demanded I be executed. They didn't just want to see me tried and convicted. They wanted an eye for an eye. They wanted my head on a platter. They wanted blood.

THE POLICE TRAINING ACADEMY where I was being held on the outskirts of Lahore shielded me from the whirlwind surrounding me, but captivity presented its own challenges. I was used to going wherever I wanted and doing whatever I pleased. That sort of freedom had been taken from me. Beyond trips to court, I was stuck inside a dank little room all day long, and there wasn't a whole lot to do. I spent hours doing pushups, squats, core workouts, and ab workouts, but there were still plenty of hours left in the day.

The visits I got from Carmela and her staff helped tremendously. At least one person from the consulate, but oftentimes more, came to see me every single day. They must have noticed I was getting bored because they always asked if they could bring me some reading material, a book perhaps, or a magazine. I'd never been a big reader, but I jumped at the chance for a diversion, something that might take my mind off my increasingly grim-looking situation, even for just a moment.

It didn't take long for me to pick up on the fact that I always got the books I requested well before the magazines. It took me a bit longer to figure out why. As I was reading a copy of British *GQ*, I noticed something odd about one of the photographs in the magazine. Something didn't look quite right. It took me a moment to realize that someone—one of the guards, most likely—had taken a black Sharpie and drawn clothes on one of the women in the photograph. Whoever had done it hadn't just hurriedly filled in the lines either. It was clear by its paint-by-numbers perfection that the illustrator had taken his time.

I flipped through the rest of the magazine and found several more examples of this covert censorship. The one that amused me the most was a photo of two women lying on a beach. Whatever revealing swimwear and bare skin they'd been displaying had been completely blacked out, and both of them were now covered in ink from their ankles all the way up to their necks.

I almost forgot sometimes that Islam, with its edicts against alcohol, drugs, extramarital sex, and homosexuality, was the state religion of Pakistan. All of these vices were successfully cracked down on in the rural villages, but in Lahore they were readily available, from the guys who would run up to your car at traffic circles trying to sell you alcohol, to the male prostitutes who would dress up as women and approach you while you were sitting at a stoplight. As a freedom-loving American, I was offended by the blacked-out photographs in the magazine, but they also made me laugh, something I hadn't done in days.

I probably got more entertainment value out of the magazines the consulate personnel brought me than anyone ever has. I read them so thoroughly I actually looked in the fine print alongside each photograph to see which kind of camera was used, the focus angle, lens type, all the information that most people gloss over. I clearly needed something more substantial to read.

The consulate personnel helped fill the void with books. I probably read more fiction during my time in captivity than I'd read during the entire thirty-six years of my life. I read like a teenager plays video games, in long, absorbing sessions that often saw me sacrificing sleep. Carmela even loaned me a book from her personal library, Pearl S. Buck's *The Good Earth*. The woman from the consulate who delivered it to me said, "You can try this one, but it's probably not your thing. You know, being a guy and all."

And she was right. It shouldn't have interested me. It was an Oprah book. Written by a woman. About life in a Chinese village. Prior to World War I. Not something I would have voluntarily read. Nor something I could ever imagine discussing with any of my SF buddies.

When the woman who'd given me the book came in the next day, I handed it back to her. "I'm done with this."

"I kinda figured you wouldn't like it. We'll try to find something that might interest you a little more."

"No, I finished it."

"You read it? The whole thing?"

"Yeah, I was up all night! I couldn't put it down. It's a great story."

The consulate personnel weren't always so spot-on with their book suggestions. I don't know how the next book they brought me ever got past the censors. Before I started reading it, I flipped to the back cover to see what it was about. "A CIA operative on the hunt for a high-value terrorist in Afghanistan . . ."

I didn't bother finishing the sentence. I hid the book under my pillow, and when the consulate personnel returned the following day I handed it back to them.

"Do you have a different book? I don't really care for this one."

"Oh, that's too bad. Why not?"

"Just read the back."

As they did, their faces drained of all color.

"When you're being accused of being a spy," I said, "reading a book about a CIA agent trying to assassinate someone doesn't seem like the smartest idea, does it?"

17.

LAHORE POLICE TRAINING COLLEGE, LAHORE, PAKISTAN
(February 10, 2011—Day 15)

A S MY FOURTEEN-DAY PHYSICAL remand neared its end, I expected
the police to become more aggressive toward me in an effort to get
me to talk, and they did. They never hit me or anything like that. They
just became much more persistent with their demands and interrogation
techniques.

"Who do you work for?" they would ask. "What is your job? Who
were the men who came after you that day? You must tell us."

But I was emphatic. "No, I'm sorry. I'm not answering any of your
questions."

They must have gotten tired of hearing me tell them the same thing
over and over, because there was a lull toward the very end during which
they didn't bother questioning me for several days. Then the night before
my physical remand was set to expire, just as I was about to fall asleep,
two guards entered my room and rousted me out of bed.

"Interview."

This was odd. I'd already spoken with the consulate personnel earlier
in the day. Maybe they'd come back because they'd forgotten to tell me
something. Maybe it was good news. Or maybe I was about to get taken
out to the woodshed. Either way, I had no real choice in the matter. I got
up and put my blue fleece on.

The guards led me downstairs, but instead of taking a left turn at the
bottom of the stairs as usual, we took a right. We walked down a hallway
I'd never seen before, and, as we came to a door at the very end of it, my
stomach churned with nervousness. In my head I'd been keeping track

of the number of days that had passed, so I knew the time the judge had given them to question me was about to run out. It was the eleventh hour, and they still hadn't gotten anything out of me other than basic facts about the incident. Knowing how frustrated they must be, I was prepared for the methods they used to interrogate me to get much harsher. The window for using the soft-sell had long passed. It was time, I suspected, for the hard-sell.

The guards opened the door, led me into the room, and pointed to a chair in the center of the room. To the left of the chair, there was a couch, and on it sat Farooq, the superintendent of the facility where I was being held; Kazmi, the officer who'd testified in court the day after the incident; and a man whose face remained hidden behind a piece of cloth. Directly in front of the chair was a desk, and three men were sitting behind it. I only recognized one of them, Officer Yaksul, the man who'd suggested that I teach his men how to shoot. Sitting to his immediate left was a man in a blue suit who referred to himself as a police officer but whom I'd never seen before. And to his left was another man I'd never seen before but wouldn't soon forget because of his distinctive getup and, I would later find out, fiery personality. He was wearing *shalwar kameez*, a traditional South Asian outfit consisting of loose-fitting, pajama-like pants (*shalwar*) and a long shirt that falls to the knees (*kameez*). He was also wearing a turban and a wrap that covered his entire face except for his eyes, so I couldn't tell exactly who he was. One of the officers told me he was a police officer, but I didn't believe it. I suspected he was ISI.

Officer Yaksul pointed at the empty chair. "Please sit down, sir."

As soon as I did, he started asking me about the incident, but I cut him off. "Look, I'm not answering any more of your questions. I'm done with this process. You have my statement."

"Why won't you answer any of our questions?"

"Because everything you need to know is in the statement I gave you. It's all there. There's no need to question me anymore. It's a waste of time."

"There are other things we need to know, sir."

"I have a diplomatic passport. The US ambassador says I have immunity. I'm being held against my will. I'm not answering any questions."

"But, sir, we need answers. It is important that—"

I stood up from my chair. "You know what? I'm done here. I'm going back to my room."

I walked over to the door and stood there and waited for one of the guards to open it. Officer Farooq got up from the couch, walked across the room, and it looked like he was about to open the door when the man in the turban yelled across the room. "You are not permitted to leave. Your place is here."

I stared at the man in the turban for a second before returning to the chair. When Officer Yaksul resumed asking questions, I cut him off.

"Do you have my passport?" I asked him.

"Yes."

"Well, all you have to do is take a look at it. It says right there on the cover that it's a diplomatic passport. I have diplomatic immunity, and I should be turned over to the diplomatic mission in Islamabad immediately. Understand?"

"But, sir, we can't release you if you won't answer our questions. Why won't you talk to us?"

"Because, to be honest, I don't know who I'm talking to." I pointed at Officer Yaksul. "I know you, sir, from the day of the incident. You were wearing a police uniform that day, so I know exactly who you are. I know Officer Kazmi because he was also there the day of the shooting, and he had a name tag on his uniform. And I know Officer Farooq. He's the officer in charge of this facility." I pointed at the man to my left whose face was hidden behind a piece of cloth. "But I don't know you." Then I pointed at the man in the blue suit. "I don't know you." Last, I pointed at the man who was wearing a turban and *shalwar kameez*. "And I don't know you."

After hearing what I'd said, the man in the turban jumped up out of his chair and started jabbing his finger at me and yelling at me. "You don't have the right to know who I am!"

I just sat there with my hands in my lap, trying to stay calm, but the man in the turban was making it awfully hard. He was standing directly over me, yelling so hard he could barely catch his breath, and his finger kept getting closer and closer to my face, so close I actually thought he was going to hit my eye. For a moment I had a flashback to SERE school. The instructors there had done this same sort of thing to me. They taught us that if we ever got into a situation like this we should never fight our captors. I could almost hear my instructor's voice, "There might only be two guards in the room with you, but you can be damn sure that there's plenty more of them on the other side of the door, more than enough to whip your ass. If you really want to know exactly how many there are, all you have to do is hit one of them, and you'll find out soon enough."

It was rare for me to let my emotions get the best of me, but this was one of those times. I was tired of being yelled at, tired of being asked to answer the same questions over and over again, and especially tired of the man in the turban jabbing his finger at my face. I knew it was a bad idea, but once the thought entered my brain I couldn't get it out: If his finger touched me, I was going to break his hand. I knew the guards would beat the hell out of me afterward, but I was going to do it anyway. I'd already made up my mind. Even the slightest amount of contact would be more than enough to provoke me. I just sat there waiting for his finger to accidentally graze my cheek, and it came *so* close to happening. It nearly hit my eyeball at one point.

The man in the turban was yelling at me so hard the cloth covering his face fell down, and for a second I could see his eyes, his mouth, even the Band-Aid stuck to the side of his nose. He hurriedly covered himself back up, but not before I was able to give him a hard time about it.

"Hey," I said through a grin so wide it threatened to reach my ears. "I saw your face."

He lost it. He started yelling at me all over again, but he was so mad he could barely get the words out. Finally, as much to catch his breath as anything, he sat back down.

When the man in the turban returned to his chair, I considered it a victory, but only a momentary one. My stubbornness and insolence combined with his anger and desperation to get information from me before my physical remand expired made for an extremely volatile mix. If these officers were going to switch tactics and try to beat the information out of me, it was, in all likelihood, going to start right now. The man's angry outburst offered a natural segue to physical violence. With the explosive energy still lingering in the room, it wouldn't have surprised me all that much if, after recovering his breath, the man walked over and punched me in the face. After all, this was it. If they failed to get me to talk tonight, they weren't going to get another chance.

Searching for a clue as to how they were going to proceed, I looked over at Officer Yaksul. His demeanor surprised me. At the same time that he was shaking his head in a scolding manner, he also appeared to be suppressing a grin. "Get him out of here," he said to the guards. "Take him back to his room. We're done here."

His words were an admission of defeat. The officers had been given ample time to question me, but they'd failed to get any sort of noteworthy information out of me. Having them give up felt like an even more substantial victory than seeing the man in the turban return to his seat, but the feeling was short-lived.

What did they have in store for me next?

18.

MODEL TOWN COURTS, LAHORE, PAKISTAN
(February 11, 2011—Day 16)

T HE ARMORED PERSONNEL CARRIER (APC) that delivered me to the courthouse the day my two-week physical remand ended must have made me look untouchable. As if its thick, steel exterior and bulletproof windows didn't offer enough protection, it was surrounded on all sides by Pakistani soldiers wielding AK-47s. But as with so many things in Pakistan, the vehicle was a bit of a charade. The truth lay at my feet, where I could see gaping holes in the thin, diamond-plate steel that covered the floor. The bottom of the vehicle wasn't armored. If we hit an IED, we were toast.

There was reason to be concerned. The pressure being placed on the Pakistani government by religious extremists who wanted me dead continued to grow. My death would remove that burden, and the trip from the police training facility to the courthouse offered a perfect opportunity. All the soldiers would have to do was look the other way as a group of "terrorists" attacked the poorly maintained APC.

The route we'd taken increased my concern. I'd gone to court so many times by this point that I'd practically memorized the directions to each of them. So when the APC turned down a street I'd never seen before, alarm bells went off in my head. Were they taking me to a different courthouse than the one I was supposed to be going to? After what I'd seen, I wouldn't have put it past the Pakistani officials to change venues at the very last second. That way, when the lawyer the consulate personnel had promised would be showing up today arrived at the wrong place, they could say, "Oh, sorry, you guys didn't get the memo?"

As far as possible explanations for the unexpected route change, that was probably the best-case scenario. The worst involved the APC suddenly turning down a dead-end street, all the soldiers running away, and me being left to defend myself against a bloodthirsty band of militants.

That's what was going through my head as the APC came to a stop in the middle of the street as we were nearing Ferozepur Road. I looked out one of the portholes on the side of the vehicle and saw the soldiers who had been walking alongside the APC take off running. Then the guard sitting in the passenger seat of the APC jumped out and did the same. I looked over at the guard sitting in the back of the vehicle with me to see how he responded. If he jumped out the back and took off running, I was going to be right on his heels. That or put up one hell of a fight.

A very long, tense moment passed before I figured out what was actually going on. The soldiers were merely breaking up a traffic jam, which had slowed our pace to a crawl. Several donkey carts were blocking the road, and the soldiers were trying to move them out of the way. One of the carts was so overloaded with goods that the donkey pulling it could barely move. The whole scene looked like something out of a cartoon, but I was too nervous to laugh.

I didn't feel much safer inside the courtroom. As usual, it was tiny, no bigger than my pickup truck back home, and it was *packed*. There were people everywhere and my hands were cuffed, and I realized that if one of them had a knife there wasn't much I'd be able to do about it.

"What is your case against Mr. Davis?" the judge asked the prosecution.

"We need more time, your honor," responded Butt.

"You had fourteen days to question him and compile evidence. You don't get any more time."

"You don't understand, your honor," interjected Officer Yaksul. "Mr. Davis is a sly and cunning individual. He eludes our questioning. We need more time to build this case."

"No, I'm sorry. You had fourteen days. That's the law. You must now present the *challan*."

In Pakistan, a *challan* is an investigative report that identifies the nature of a crime, the identity of the accused, and the testimony of any witnesses. After a police officer submitted one that accused me of murdering the two men who'd ambushed me, the prosecutor took the opportunity to review one of the most sensational aspects of the report, and, just as in previous court visits, it represented a radical deviation from the truth.

"Your honor, Mr. Davis was running wildly down the street shooting innocent people."

Luckily, a local lawyer named Hassam Qadir had shown up on my behalf, but all he did was submit an application contending that I enjoyed diplomatic immunity and requested that my trial be held *in camera*, that is, in private with the public and press prohibited from viewing the proceedings. Because I'd never seen him before and because his English wasn't the best, he didn't make me feel all that comfortable and I doubted that he was the solution to my problem.

I had much more confidence in Samir, who had become indispensable as far as helping me navigate the treacherous waters of the Pakistani court system. I was still getting screwed at every turn, but at least now, thanks to Samir's translations, I had a much better understanding of how the screwing was being done.

"Seriously?" I said to Samir. "That's a complete fabrication. How can they get away with this crap?"

"Hey, man, don't worry about it."

The judge asked me how I was going to plead, and I said, "Not guilty."

The judge turned to the prosecution. "Do you have anything else to add?"

"No, sir."

He looked at me. "Do you have anything to add?"

"I have diplomatic immunity and should be released immediately."

"That is never going to happen," Butt said, barely containing the disdain in his voice. "You killed two defenseless men in cold blood. You are a vicious dog and will be treated as such."

"What did he just call me?" I asked Samir.

"Let it go, Ray."

But I couldn't. I barely heard the judge as he issued a fourteen-day judicial remand for me and set my next court date for February 25. From what I'd been told about the Pakistani legal system, I should have been, if not rejoicing, then at least mildly pleased about this development. Because Pakistan doesn't have any sort of speedy trial law or plea bargaining, trials can take years to complete, while those being tried waste away in prison.

My case seemed to be on somewhat of a fast track, but I was so angry about what Butt had said that I could barely process this development.

A policeman took me by the arm and started to lead me out of the room. "We must go now, sir."

"No, I need to have a word with that prosecutor."

Samir stepped in front of me. "No, you don't, Ray."

"Yeah, I'm pretty sure I do."

Samir grabbed me and steered me toward the door, a remarkable feat for someone I outweighed by a good seventy pounds. "You need to mellow out, man. C'mon, let's get out of here."

With his calm, authoritative demeanor, Samir had helped me avoid a confrontation that I surely would have regretted. But, unfortunately, he couldn't do anything to change my fate.

After thirty-six years of clean living, without so much as a single visit to the principal's office or even a ticket for doing 75 in a 65 mph speed zone, I was going to prison.

BUILT TO HOUSE 4,000 PRISONERS, Lahore's notorious Kot Lakhpat Jail actually contained more than four times that number, as well as an exponentially greater amount of violence compared to that found just outside its walls. Numerous prisoners had been killed here, by one another, by guards, and by court-ordered hangings. This was where hope, redemption, and convicted terrorists came to die.

As hard as I imagine it would be to escape such a place, it was nearly as difficult to enter. There was an airport-security-style metal detector at the entrance, and the guards who manned it made me take off my jacket, shoes, and belt and ran each item through the machine. Then they checked every seam of the jacket to make sure nothing had been hidden in the lining, even going so far as to bend the fabric back and forth. Next they ran my bag of possessions through the metal detector. After it came out the other end, they took everything out of the bag and ran each item, one by one, back through the metal detector. As my possessions made their way down the conveyor belt, the guard standing at the end picked them up and examined them as if they were alien artifacts. He even sniffed a pen I had, checking for who knows what. When I'd arrived at the prison, I'd seen a clock on the wall that said it was 11:30 A.M. By the time that absurdly long and overly thorough check-in process was finally completed, it was 12:30 P.M.

Two guards led me, still in handcuffs, down a long hall and through an enormous steel door that was nearly the same height and width as the hallway. The door looked like something you might see in an old James Bond movie, and it was shut tight. There was a smaller door within the big door, and to get through it you needed to step over a barrier and duck at the same time. Beyond this door was a large room partitioned with wooden office dividers. There were three cubicles on the right and three on the left and a walkway between them down the center. The guards told me to have a seat in the chair in one of the cubicles.

"Okay, sir, we need to get your fingerprints," said the officer sitting behind the desk.

"No, you don't."

I wished I could have taken a picture of the look on his face, a mixture of astonishment and disbelief. "You cannot refuse."

"Sure, I can. I'm with the US Embassy. I have diplomatic immunity. It's illegal for you to detain me. You need to turn me over to the US dip-lomatic mission in Islamabad right now."

Ignoring me, the officer went back to his paperwork. "Please tell me your mother's name, sir."

"No, I'm sorry. I'm not answering any of your questions."

The officer tried several more times, but my responses remained the same. His frustration eventually made itself known when he let a long sigh escape his mouth. "Fine. I will discuss this matter with your consul-ate's staff when they arrive later today. You can refuse to cooperate, but I promise we will get the information we seek soon enough." He gestured to the guards standing behind me. "Take him to his cell."

We exited the main building and walked across a courtyard. Along the way, I noticed that the perimeter of the building we'd just left wasn't lined with concertina wire and its walls weren't all that high, either. The idea briefly occurred to me that with just two quick steps I could run and jump and grab the top edge of the wall, Jackie Chan style, and pull myself up and over. It appeared to be that easy. But, of course, there was no way of knowing what was on the other side. These are the kind of thoughts that enter your head when you're in prison. Unless you're crazy, all you can think about is how to get the hell out of there.

This feeling intensified when I walked into my cell. It was rectangular, roughly seven yards by three yards, and contained a desk and a chair and a thin mattress only slightly more comfortable than the concrete floor it lay upon. Off to the right was a bathroom with a sink, a mirror, and a little tub that reminded me of one of those inflatable swimming pools for little kids. The plumbing was gravity-fed. Any water used in the sink and tub came from a tank on the roof, and it was always the same temperature: ice cold. As basic as the amenities were, the room did have one high-tech feature: a camera in the main part of the room and one in the bathroom, so no matter where I went, the guards could always keep an eye on me.

When asked about the cameras, the superintendent of the prison, an older man who was several inches shorter than me, sported a hefty paunch, and spoke fairly good English, said they were for my own protection, a "safeguard" put into place to ensure that I went unharmed while I was being held there. There were other safeguards. Several hundred Punjabi Rangers had been brought in and placed in a protective ring around the prison. I was housed in a special section of the prison that was isolated from its general population, while the twenty-five terrorists who'd been living there were transferred to other facilities, giving me an entire wing to myself. And the guards who monitored my cell weren't allowed to carry weapons. The superintendent made it sound as if all of these measures had been put in place to protect me, but it seemed just as clear to me that they were also designed to thwart any rescue attempts.

When the guard closed the door to my cell and locked me inside, a jolt of anxiety shot through me. Up to this point in my life, I'd never been in trouble. I'd never been arrested, and I'd certainly never been in jail. Hearing the door lock behind me was like a kick in the gut. My freedom had just been taken from me. Someone else was now in complete control of me. I was trapped behind a locked door, prevented from coming and going as I pleased. It was an awful feeling. I now know what a caged tiger feels like. For the next eight hours, I never stopped moving. At one point, the guards brought me a pizza, but I was too distraught to eat it. All I could do was pace around and around the room as all sorts of terrible thoughts went through my head. I was convinced that I was going to be in there until I was old and gray and that I was never going to see my wife or son again.

If that were to happen, I knew Rebecca would understand. She would obviously be upset, but she'd been in the military and she was an adult, so at least she'd be able to get her head around the idea. But how do you explain something like that to a little kid? You couldn't, and knowing that only made it worse. I'd been looking forward to teaching my son how to fly a kite and throw a football, taking him to the pool on hot summer days, and walking him to school on his first day of kindergarten. Now the simple pleasure of watching my son grow up, something so many of us take for granted, began to seem more like a remote possibility, and let me tell you, there's no worse feeling than that.

19.

CONSUL GENERAL'S RESIDENCE, LAHORE, PAKISTAN

(February 15, 2011—Day 20)

W HEN PAKISTAN WAS CREATED IN 1947, the portion of the British Indian Army it inherited was much bigger than the newly established country could afford to maintain, but much smaller, its leaders decided, than what was needed to protect itself from India. The prudent move would have been to downsize the army. Instead, fueled by a nagging fear of its rival, it set about expanding it. At one point in the 1950s, Pakistan was devoting more than 60 percent of its national budget to its military. Despite having almost no industry to speak of, the fledgling country appeared far more interested in protecting its borders than it was in growing its economy.

To help Pakistan get on its feet during the first year of its existence, the United States gave it $10 million in aid, and in exchange it received assurances that Pakistan would help protect the strategic interests of the United States in the region. The terms of their dysfunctional, almost codependent, but amazingly long-lasting relationship had been set: In exchange for money (and later, weapons) Pakistan delivered some vague, ever-changing geopolitical benefits. During the Cold War, that meant acting as a buffer against the Soviet Union and the spread of communism. During the Soviet War in Afghanistan, that meant providing a base from which the CIA could train and fund the *mujahedin*. And during the War on Terror, that meant occasionally hunting down a member of al-Qaeda.

For Pakistan, no amount of money ever seemed to be enough. The economic aid it received from the United States became a drug it alternately loathed and couldn't live without. Between 1954 and 1959, the

United States gave Pakistan $1.28 billion. By 2011, the total amount of aid doled out by the United States had ballooned to $67 billion. After 9/11, the United States, using Coalition Support Funds, also reimbursed Pakistan for any money it spent combating terrorism, a policy that was somewhat flawed because, while it was supposed to encourage the Pakistani military to fight local militants, it provided little incentive for it to do the job well. After all, if all the terrorists disappeared, so too would the seemingly limitless ATM that was the United States. Having grown dependent upon these annual disbursements of aid from the United States and with fewer than two million of its 182 million citizens paying income tax, Pakistan had become the very definition of a "rentier state," a country that receives a disproportionate amount of its revenues from external sources, kind of like the ne'er-do-well child of fabulously wealthy parents.

As dysfunctional as the relationship between the United States and Pakistan was, it was made worse by the fact that most of the aid typically ended up in the hands of the Pakistani military, while much of its population continued to languish in poverty. In 2009, Senator John Kerry set about changing that.

Kerry had always been committed to the welfare of the region and the hope of seeing democracy flourish there. He'd visited Afghanistan during the run-up to its presidential election in 2004—I was actually on the team assigned to protect him—and he'd flown to Pakistan for much the same reason in 2008, observing firsthand the presidential election that saw Asif Ali Zardari replace the military dictator Pervez Musharraf.

After replacing Joe Biden as the chairman of the Senate Foreign Relations Committee in 2009, Kerry became even more involved in Pakistani affairs, visiting the country four times and using his influence, along with that of Senator Richard Lugar (R–Indiana) and Representative Howard Berman (D–California), to get the Enhanced Partnership with Pakistan Act passed. This aid package, which promised Pakistan $7.5 billion over the course of five years, was intended to heal the growing rift between the two countries and improve the welfare of the Pakistani people by investing in the country's health care, education, and social services. More than a third of the Pakistani population was living below the poverty line and, thanks to an outmoded and failing electrical grid, many of them were forced to do without electricity for the majority of the day.

If this legislation was meant to be an olive branch, many Pakistanis reacted as if the United States had slapped them in the face with it. While President Zardari supported it, nearly everyone else in Pakistan was angered by what they considered to be its insulting language and insinuations. "Kerry-Lugar triples civilian aid to Pakistan," the outspoken journalist and politician Ayaz Amir editorialized in Pakistan's largest English-language newspaper, *The News International*, "but on terms and conditions that amount to a ten-fold increase in national humiliation."

The Pakistani military was even more incensed, citing "serious concern" about clauses in the bill that required it to submit to greater US oversight. Any assistance it would now receive would be based on how effective it was at combating the Taliban and al-Qaeda militants operating inside Pakistan's borders. The bill also threatened to cut off the aid if the military ever staged a coup.

Three days before President Obama was to sign the Enhanced Partnership with Pakistan Act into law, Pakistan's foreign minister, Shah Mahmood Qureshi, flew to Washington to relay the Pakistani military's concerns. Kerry had always enjoyed a close working relationship with Qureshi. He often referred to him as a friend, and he'd even given Qureshi's son Zain an internship in his Senate office.

But when Kerry flew to Pakistan on February 15, 2011, to attempt to broker a deal that might spring me from the Lahore prison where I was being detained on judicial remand, Qureshi didn't act like much of a friend. Rather than giving in to the government's wish that I be granted diplomatic immunity, he'd actually resigned his position three days after the incident at Mozang Chowk, and two weeks later he remained undeterred. In a meeting of top Pakistani officials, both President Zardari and Prime Minister Gilani tried to convince Qureshi to change his hardline stance, but Qureshi let it be known in a press conference the following day that he wasn't going to budge.

"It is time to not bow down before the US and the need of the hour is to live with raised heads," he said. "If summoned by the court, I will give my opinion with honesty. God willing, I will side with the truth. I will never disappoint the nation."

During his two-day visit to Pakistan, Kerry also met with Zardari, Gilani, and the army chief, General Kayani, and in an informal press conference at Carmela Conroy's consular residence in Lahore, he addressed the Pakistani media. Sitting in a lounge chair flanked by houseplants, Kerry expressed regret over the deaths of the three Pakistani civilians but didn't give an inch when it came to discussing my status as a diplomat who should be granted immunity.

"It is the strong belief of our government that this case does not belong in the court," he said, "and it does not belong in the court because this man has diplomatic immunity as an administrative, technical employee of the Embassy of the United States in Islamabad, and we believe the documentation makes that clear."

During the press conference, Kerry did everything but get down on one knee. He expressed sympathy for the families of the three dead men. He emphasized his involvement in the country, highlighting his contribution to the Kerry–Lugar–Berman bill and his visit the previous summer in the wake of devastating floods. He quoted the Prophet Muhammad and recognized that the celebration of his birthday was imminent. He assured everyone present that the US Department of Justice (DOJ) would be conducting a criminal investigation into the shooting. And he stressed the importance of looking at the big picture instead of focusing on one incendiary event:

> I'm not trying to dismiss this incident. We honor what it means. But we need to reach beyond it and find a way to go forward and not have this become something that tears us apart. I'm confident there's a way to do that. But it requires all of our politicians—yours and ours—to step back and take a look at the whole relationship. And we also, all of us, have to respect the law. This is not a law the United States wrote. This is not a law that Pakistan idly signed up to. Your leaders signed up to this long, long ago. We didn't create this; we live with it. And it's important for us to live with it because there are incidents that occur sometimes in one part of the world or another where diplomats are not able to do the job they're called on to do, in very dangerous circumstances sometimes, unless they have that immunity. That was decided by the global community fifty years ago.

Toward the end of the press conference, as Kerry began to stray from his prepared remarks and grew more candid with the journalists, he seemed to have a personal revelation about the place my case had in the grand scheme of things, as the Pakistani–US relationship continued its downward trajectory and the revolutionary fervor of the Arab Spring persisted.

"You know the challenges we face. This is as complex and dangerous of a time in the world as I've seen in all of my time in public life. The world is changing. And we've seen that in the last weeks very evidently. It's changing because people want their hopes and dreams fulfilled. Our job in public life is to try to help do that."

AT NEARLY THE SAME TIME Kerry was speaking, President Obama addressed my situation during a press conference held in the South Court Auditorium of the Eisenhower Executive Office Building. Most of the questions lobbed at the president during the hour-long affair had to do with the budget deficit and recent events in the Middle East, but in the latter half of a two-part question *ABC News* correspondent Jake Tapper asked what the United States was doing about my situation.

"With respect to Mr. Davis, our diplomat in Pakistan," Obama responded, "we've got a very simple principle here that every country in the world that is party to the Vienna Convention on Diplomatic Relations has upheld in the past and should uphold in the future, and that is if our diplomats are in another country, then they are not subject to that country's local prosecution."

Obama went on to explain why he was willing to take a hard line on this issue. "The reason this is an important principle is if it starts being fair game on our ambassadors around the world, including in dangerous places, where we may have differences with those governments, and our ambassadors or our various embassy personnel are having to deliver tough messages to countries where we disagree with them on X, Y, Z, and they start being vulnerable to prosecution locally, that's untenable. It means they can't do their job. And that's why we respect these conventions, and every country should as well."

That same day, the Pakistani Taliban (TTP) released an equally tough statement commenting about my situation. "If [Pakistani] rulers hand him over to America, then we will target these rulers," said TTP spokesman Azam Tariq. "If Pakistani courts cannot punish Davis, then they should hand him over to us. We will give exemplary punishment to the killer Davis."

With all parties involved drawing lines in the sand, the issue was only getting more complicated, more heated, and, unfortunately for me, more removed from a possible solution.

20.

KOT LAKHPAT JAIL, LAHORE, PAKISTAN
(February 16, 2011—Day 21)

W HEN YOU'RE KEPT IN ISOLATION all but two hours each day without a watch or clock to anchor you in time, you start to feel a little
disconnected from reality, and no amount of training can adequately
prepare you for it. I suppose that explains how I started talking to animals.

There were two little birds that flew into my cell from time to time,
and I named them Margaret and George. They would hop around the
floor looking for any scraps of food I might have dropped and eye me
warily. I would do my best not to spook them, but it didn't matter. They
never stuck around very long before taking off.

Larry was a more reliable and sociable visitor. Larry was a lizard that
lived in the cracks of the wall. I'd be reading a book, and I'd spot something out of the corner of my eye, and I'd look up to see Larry slithering
across the wall.

"How's it going today, Larry?" I'd ask.

Sometimes he'd freeze and look in my direction. More often he'd
continue on his way, darting in and out of cracks in the wall in search of
whatever sustained him: crickets, flies, spiders.

When I wasn't having conversations with animals, I could often be
found working out, doing pushups, squats, anything I could think of to
help me stay in shape and pass the time. With its concrete floors and lack
of heat, my cell was always extremely cold, but I would work out so hard
I'd actually work up a sweat, and afterward I'd go into the bathroom, fill
up the little tub, and wash off. There was a camera in the bathroom, but
whenever I spent any length of time in there the guards would still come

check on me. I can't tell you how many times I'd be bent over in the tub splashing water on myself, and I'd turn around and see a handful of guards staring at me from the window with a kind of slack-jawed wonder. It was a little creepy and very annoying.

Even more irritating were the times they'd barge right into my cell and make certain requests of me, requests that came out sounding more like demands. They'd say, "We want you to wear *shalwar kameez*."

Or: "We need to fingerprint you."

Or: "You need to give us information about your family."

I'd gotten very good at stonewalling them. "I'm sure the consulate personnel would be happy to address your concerns," I'd say. "Please take it up with them."

As if the consulate personnel didn't have enough to do already. They continued to visit me nearly every single day and were constantly lobbying the prison superintendent on my behalf. They asked if I could use a jump rope in my cell. The superintendent denied this request because he said I might hang myself with it. They asked if I could have a clock. He said he would look into it. They asked if the loudspeaker just outside my cell that blared music and sermons round the clock on *Eid Milad un-Nabi*, the celebration of the Prophet Muhammad's birthday, could be moved. He actually granted this request, and thank god, because it was driving me crazy. Noise blasted out of that speaker for five straight days. There would be a call to prayer, followed by a fiery sermon that reminded me of a Baptist minister preaching about hell, followed by music, then another call to prayer. And then the cycle would repeat itself.

From time to time, the consulate personnel would also bring me snacks such as crackers or cookies or M&Ms. After being forced to eat chicken curry and rice every single meal, I started to really look forward to these treats, but then one day, the superintendent demanded an end to the care packages. "There will be no more food coming in," he said.

Evidently, I had a counterterrorist expert, who was asked on Pakistani television to name some of the ways the United States might try to break me out of the prison, to thank for that. One of the scenarios he described involved a US government official slipping me a drug that would make me appear deathly ill but wouldn't actually kill me. I would have to be removed from the prison and taken to a hospital, and along the way a

Special Operations team would swoop in, stop the vehicle, grab me, and hustle me out of the country.

Once the superintendent caught wind of this idea, he barred the consulate personnel from bringing me any more food. "There's only one person who will be handling your food from now on," he told me. "This man will buy it, prepare it, and bring it to you. He's the only one who will ever touch your food. If anyone else gives you something to eat, do not eat it. Understand?"

It was even rumored that dogs tasted my food before it was brought to me to ensure that it hadn't been poisoned, although I had a hard time believing it because in Pakistan, as in most countries where Islam is the predominant religion, dogs are considered unclean.

For all that the consulate personnel did for me, I valued nothing more than their company. Their visits helped break up the monotony of my days and, quite often, were the highlights of those days. I especially enjoyed my time with Samir. When we talked, it was like talking to one of my old SF buddies. He was somebody I could see myself hanging out with back home. We would talk for hours and hours, and it was rarely about the incident. In fact, it was usually about *anything other than* the incident. One day we'd talk about the Super Bowl—I heard that the Packers had beaten the Steelers after Pittsburgh failed to score on its final drive. Another day we'd talk about what was going on in the Middle East.

Samir was just a really nice, really genuine guy who more than anyone else seemed to understand the importance of taking my mind off of what was going on. When the conversation during one of my meetings with the consulate personnel started heading in an overly serious direction one afternoon, he suggested we each tell a joke. This idea was met with silence as we racked our brains, trying to recall some humorous one-liner, or looked for ways to avoid participating, until Carmela, who was typically so reserved and businesslike, suddenly exclaimed, "I've got one!"

All heads turned her way.

"A rope walks into a bar and says, 'Hey, bartender, give me a drink.' The bartender says, 'We don't serve ropes. Get out of here.' So the rope goes outside and ties himself into a knot and frays both of his ends. He goes back into the bar and says, 'Hey, bartender, can I get a drink now?' and the bartender goes, 'Aren't you that rope I just kicked out of here?'

and the rope says, 'No, I'm a frayed knot.'" As she was saying this, she wrapped her arms around her chest and adopted a frightened expression. "*Afraid not*,'" she repeated.

It was just a silly kid's joke, but the way she did it, acting it out and changing her voice for each of the characters, she nearly had us rolling on the floor.

THE NEXT TIME THE CONSULATE PERSONNEL visited I didn't hold back when they asked me how I was doing. "Good. Real good. Margaret and George visited me this morning."

Carmela shot me a strange look. "Margaret and George?"

"Yeah, these two little birds fly into my room from time to time. Their visit was the highlight of my morning. Then Larry the Lizard came, and I didn't know what to do with myself. Back-to-back visitors. It was almost too much."

They laughed, but it seemed more nervous than genuine.

"So I've been in this prison for almost a week. What's going on? What are you-all doing to get me out of here?"

"Ray, we're doing everything we can," said Carmela. "You just need to continue being patient."

"Have you-all found another lawyer for me yet?"

When Hassam Qadir, the lawyer who'd represented me during my appearance in the Model Town Courts the week before, suddenly quit just a few days after being hired, it had opened a gaping hole in my defense team. I could be patient about many things, but waiting days and days just to get legal representation while I was on trial for murder wasn't one of them.

"We're still working on that," she said. "It's going to happen. I promise you. Your case is getting every bit of the attention it deserves. It's actually being discussed at the highest level of government."

"Yeah, all right, but can you tell me what *exactly* is being done? I'm starting to feel like I'm being forgotten about in here."

"Oh, no, please don't think that. Because that is certainly not the case. Senator Kerry arrived here yesterday to help figure out a way to get you released. He held a press conference that was aired live on every channel in the country. And as I said, your situation has been—and I'm sure will continue to be—discussed at the highest level of government."

"*The highest level of government,* huh? What does that even mean?"

"The president, Ray. Your name has appeared in the PDB."

That got my attention. The PDB, or Presidential Daily Brief, was a highly classified document given to the president each morning by the director of national intelligence in an effort to keep the president up to date about the most pressing intelligence and national security issues facing our nation. To give you an idea of just how important this document is, know that on August 6, 2001, President George W. Bush received a PDB that included the headline, "Bin Ladin Determined to Strike in US." Similar warnings had been previously issued during Bush's time in office as well as during Bill Clinton's presidency, and while they obviously weren't ignored, they also weren't acted upon to the degree that hindsight suggests they should have been.

I wasn't sure if having my name appear in the PDB was a good thing or a bad thing. "The PDB, huh? Well, that's something, I guess."

"I don't think you understand how much attention your situation is getting, Ray. The president actually commented about it in a press conference yesterday. That's how big this has gotten. So please trust me—you're definitely not being ignored."

ON THE WAY BACK TO MY CELL, during a brief stretch where I was allowed to walk outside, I got caught in a hailstorm. The pellets weren't very big. They were actually quite small. But they were coming down *hard.*

I didn't care. Whenever I got a chance to be outside, I always walked as slowly as I could, savoring every second of fresh air and natural light that I could, but on this day I walked *really* slowly. The guards on either side of me were yelling at me to hurry up, but I just used my left arm to shield my face from the hail and continued to walk at my own leisurely pace. Doing this was a way for me to assume some measure of control over my situation, and, in the ongoing battle between the prison staff and myself over my personal freedoms, I considered it a major triumph.

When I got back to my cell, I discovered that I'd won another battle while I'd been away. On the wall way up high was the clock the consulate personnel had asked that I be allowed to have. I lay down on my mattress, content just to stare at it, and as I did the lizard appeared. It was running horizontally across the wall until it discovered that the usual path it took was now blocked by a large, circular object. The lizard stopped and stared at the clock as if trying to make sense of it.

"What are you doing, Larry?"

The lizard turned its head and looked at me.

"Please be careful around my new clock. After all the work Carmela and them put into getting it, it would be a real shame if you knocked it off the wall and broke it. You hear me?"

The lizard darted into a crack that led behind the clock, and as it did the clock wobbled a little.

I ran across the room so fast you would have thought my pants were on fire. I reached up to steady the clock with my hands, and as I did, I saw the name of the company that had made it: Victory. Which, to my ears, sounded just about right. That single word captured how I felt at that moment so perfectly I couldn't help but grin.

21.

KOT LAKHPAT JAIL, LAHORE, PAKISTAN
(February 17, 2011—Day 22)

F OR EVERY SMALL VICTORY I earned while I was in prison, it seemed there were twice as many setbacks. It didn't bother me all that much that I was fed the same pasty gruel every single day, and I got used to sleeping on a hopelessly thin mattress on the concrete floor with the overhead light constantly on. I even learned to tolerate getting ogled while I was bathing. But the little mind games the prison staff played with me, the basic theme of which was, "We control you and everything you have," quickly got under my skin.

Here's an example of what I'm talking about: One day a guard came into my cell, grabbed my notepad, and said, "I don't know if this is authorized, sir. I'm going to have to take it and see."

I thought this was very strange because I was under the impression that all my possessions had already been approved during the painfully long check-in process. Anything I wasn't supposed to have, such as my watch and phone, had already been confiscated. But I didn't worry too much about it because I hadn't written anything in the notepad and had no immediate plans to start.

The guard returned the notepad later that day and said, "It's okay for you to have this, sir. It has been approved."

He set it on the table before grabbing my writing utensils, a pencil and a pen. "Now I must check on these items, sir. I need to make sure you're authorized to have them."

He took them and left.

I wasn't too bothered by this, either, until he came back, set the writing utensils down on the table, and grabbed one of my books.

"It's okay for you to have these writing implements, sir, but I don't know about this book. I must take it and see if it has been authorized. I will—"

I cut him off. "Look, I see the little game you're playing here, and you know what? I refuse to be a part of it. Screw it. You can take everything I have. I don't care." He flinched as I pointed my finger at him. "But know this. If you take my stuff from me, I neither require, nor do I need, anything else from you. If you continue to take my things from me, I will refuse to accept anything you try to give me, and that includes food. Understand?"

Did I have a plan? Not really. I just wanted to show them that, despite their efforts to prove otherwise, there were some things in my life I could control and the most obvious one to me was food. I didn't have to eat anything they gave me if I didn't want to. I'd been taught that if I were ever in a situation like this my captors might start manipulating my diet to show they were in control by giving me smaller and smaller amounts of food. But how much you eat is really up to you, isn't it? Up to this point, I'd eaten sparingly. From this point forward, I didn't eat at all.

That night when the man who prepared my food brought me dinner, I pushed the tray aside. "No, thank you," I told him. "I don't want it."

When he returned in the morning with my next meal, he found the one from the night before still sitting on the floor, untouched. He set the new tray down and took the old one away.

That night, same thing.

The next morning, same thing.

This went on for three days.

Finally, the prison doctor visited my cell. "I've heard that you've stopped eating. Why are you doing this?"

"I'm glad you asked. The guards have been coming into my cell and taking my stuff and saying it needs to be authorized, but everything I have has already been approved or else it wouldn't be in here, now would it? Well, I refuse to play these little games with them. If you-all want my stuff so badly, go ahead and take it. Take it all. I don't require, nor do I need, anything from you."

Despite how well he spoke English, he didn't seem to understand exactly what I was saying. The idea that someone would refuse to eat seemed completely foreign to him. He gestured at the tray of food on the floor. "I will eat with you. How about that?"

"I told you. I don't want any food."

"But you must be hungry. It's been three days."

"No, I'm fine. Thank you." He ate a handful of rice and looked up at me. "You're not going to make me eat by myself, are you?"

"If you're hungry, go ahead. You can have it all. Knock yourself out. Like I said, I'm not eating." The doctor jerked upright as if struck by a thought. "Do you know why you're not eating? I think you might be lonely."

"Lonely?"

"Yes, lonely. You're in here all by yourself most of the day. It must be very hard. But we have people from all over the world in this prison. France, New Zealand, India, Zimbabwe. All kinds of people. Interesting people. We could bring in one or two of them to keep you company. That way you wouldn't be alone."

He was trying to portray these men as good companions with whom I might pass the time playing cards and chitchatting about world events, but I envisioned thugs and assassins who would be rewarded for killing me while I slept. "No, thank you. I prefer to be alone. You're not putting anyone in this cell with me. Do you understand? I don't need company. I don't need food. I don't need anything from you people."

Once again, he didn't seem to understand the point I was trying to make. That or he just didn't want to. We sat in silence for what seemed a really long time until he finally turned to me and, apropos of nothing, said, "Do you know who Aafia Siddiqui is?"

I nodded warily. How could I not know who Aafia Siddiqui was? Dubbed "Lady al-Qaeda" by the press, she was, until her arrest in 2008, a fixture on the FBI's Most Wanted Terrorists list. How she ended up on that list after spending the first half of her life as a gifted academic remains somewhat of a mystery.

Born and raised in Karachi, Siddiqui moved from Pakistan to the United States in 1990 to study at the University of Houston. After moving to Boston, where she completed her undergraduate studies at the Massachusetts Institute of Technology, she went on to get a PhD in cognitive neuroscience from Brandeis University. She had always been a devout Muslim, but while living in Boston her devotion took on a militant tone as she became an activist for a variety of Islamic causes and organizations. One of them was the Al Kifah Refugee Center in Brooklyn, New York, which, it would later be discovered, had direct ties to al-Qaeda.

As it was for so many others, 9/11 seems to have been a turning point in her life. In June 2002, she and her then-husband were questioned by the FBI regarding a $10,000 Internet purchase of night vision goggles, body armor, and more than fifty military manuals that included such eyebrow-raising titles as *The Anarchist's Arsenal* and *How to Make C-4*. She and her husband divorced four months later, and the following year she moved back to Pakistan and onto the FBI's Most Wanted list.

Siddiqui wasn't heard from again until July 17, 2008, when she was arrested in Ghazni, Afghanistan, by local police who found in the bag she was carrying notes explaining how to make weapons of mass destruction. She was also carrying numerous toxic chemicals, including two pounds of sodium cyanide. While being questioned the following day, she grabbed a US Army warrant officer's rifle, yelled, "Get the fuck out of here!" and fired two shots at him and a captain who was also in the room. The warrant officer returned fire with a 9-millimeter pistol, hitting her in the stomach, before a translator who was in the room was able to disarm her.

After an eighteen-month-long detention in New York and a fourteen-day trial in which she came off sounding deranged—she refused to work with the two public defenders assigned to her case because they were Jewish, demanded that Jews not be allowed on the jury, and had to be removed from the courtroom several times for shouting during the proceedings—she was convicted of attempted murder and sentenced to eighty-six years in a federal prison in Fort Worth, Texas.

To Americans who were familiar with her story, Siddiqui was nothing more than a failed terrorist and a bit of a nut job as well, but in Pakistan she came to be viewed as a martyr and a symbol of America's heavy-handedness in the region. The Pakistani government and people would welcome her back with open arms. So it didn't surprise me when the doctor suggested the idea of a prisoner exchange.

"If you can get your people to let her go, it would pave the way for your own release," he told me. "You could probably be out of here within a day or so."

"Really?"

"Yes, certainly. All you have to do is get your people to agree to that arrangement."

"Let me see if I understand this correctly. If I get them to release Aafia Siddiqui, then I'm out of here as well?"

"That is correct."

"All right, I'll see what I can do."

LATER THAT DAY, the prison superintendent paid a visit to my cell while I was talking with Samir. Samir and I were enjoying another one of our long, meandering conversations that succeeded in taking my mind off the fact that I was imprisoned in a foreign country. I never did catch Samir's official job title, but I wouldn't have been surprised if it had something to do with prison welfare or social work. He was that good at setting me at ease.

Samir and the superintendent had a brief exchange in Urdu after which Samir turned to me and asked, "What's this about you refusing to eat?"

"It's no big deal. I just needed to send them a message. They've been coming in and taking my stuff, things that have already been authorized to be here. I know they're doing it just to mess with my head, but I refuse to play these little mind games with them. It's stressful. If they want my stuff, they can have it. They can take it all. I don't need anything from them, and that includes food. They can't force me to eat. They can't make me do anything. To hell with them."

"But, Ray, you've got to eat. Here, let me explain to him what's going on."

Samir resumed speaking with the superintendent in Urdu. They went back and forth, occasionally gesturing in my direction or at some of my possessions on the table. By the end of the exchange both of them were smiling.

"Okay," Samir said to me. "He gets it now. He's going to put a stop to the guards taking your stuff. Will you start eating now?"

"If they're going to leave my stuff alone and stop messing with me, yeah, sure."

"Well, all right then." Samir made an imaginary phone out of his hand, with his thumb pressed against one ear and his pinky hovering over his mouth, and he started speaking into it with the privileged tone of a guest in a fancy hotel. "Room service, please. Can you send up a couple T-bone steaks and a six-pack of beer? My good friend Ray and I are celebrating his return to the land of the living!"

22.

KOT LAKHPAT JAIL, LAHORE, PAKISTAN
(February 19, 2011—Day 24)

I WAS TOLD I HAD VISITORS from the consulate waiting to see me in the meeting room. These visits had become such an integral part of my daily routine I almost took them for granted at times, but this particular one, from its inauspicious beginning to its fiery end, was anything but routine.

As I was passing through the small door that was set within the enormous steel door on my way to the meeting, I failed to properly execute the required maneuver—stepping over a foot-tall rise and ducking my head at the same time—and I slammed the top of my head against the door frame. I hit it so hard the door shook. The sound echoed down the hall, and it was loud. The blow stunned me, making my eyes water and nearly dropping me to my knees. When I walked into the room where I'd been questioned the first day, my eyes were still watery and red, so it must have looked like I'd been crying.

Carmela was talking to the superintendent of the prison and a man from the Punjab Home Department, which, as far as I could tell, was the Pakistani version of the State Department, but as soon as she saw me and the condition I was in, she popped out of her chair and hurried over to me.

"Are you all right, Ray?"

I knew I must have looked like I was in bad shape, but, to be honest, she didn't look that much better. After opening up her home for John Kerry's late-night press conference, visiting me nearly every single day for the past three weeks, and working around the clock to help resolve my predicament—all this in addition to the normal demands of her extremely challenging job—she looked, and surely was, exhausted.

"I'll be fine," I told her. "Just bumped my head on the door coming in. Nothing but a stupid accident. You're the one who looks like they could use some help. You look exhausted. Why don't you go get some rest? You really don't need to be coming in here all the time. Let someone else do it. Or don't bother sending anyone at all. It's not like I'm going anywhere. I'll still be here when you come back."

"Oh, Ray, you're such a protector. We're supposed to be helping you, but you're always giving us advice. Don't you worry about me. I'll be fine." She gave my arm a comforting squeeze and returned to her seat. "I hear you've resumed eating. That's good. You're not going to be doing that again, I hope."

I shrugged.

"And how about sleep?" she asked. "You getting enough?"

"Of course he is," said the superintendent. "He is getting most excellent care. He is probably treated better than any prisoner here. He gets special treatment all the time, but we must remember he is no different from the others. We have rules here, and he must follow them. He should be wearing *shalwar kameez* just as the other prisoners do."

A former prosecutor, Carmela had a way of projecting a sense of power and confidence. She made it clear by her posture—spine straight as a flag pole, gaze penetrating and direct—that she was in no way intimidated by the superintendent. "I'm sorry," she responded kindly but emphatically. "But he will not be wearing *shalwar kameez*. Despite what you say, he is not like the other prisoners here. He is being held in violation of the laws set forth in the 1961 Vienna Convention on Diplomatic Relations. Mr. Davis has diplomatic immunity and needs to be handed over to the diplomatic mission in Islamabad. Until that time, he will continue to wear the clothes he has."

"Very well. Let's continue to discuss our need to have his fingerprints taken. Mr. Davis is a prisoner here after all, and all prisoners are required to be fingerprinted and to provide certain basic information upon being processed into this prison. He has repeatedly refused to do this, which is in violation of our prison's rules."

"I understand the importance of this," said Carmela. "And I promise I'm working to resolve this issue. I'm just waiting to hear from our government whether, due to the particular circumstances of this case, he does in fact have to provide that information or not."

I was happy to hear her stonewalling the prison staff, just as I had been ever since I'd set foot in the prison. Every day, sometimes as often as two or three times a day, they would ask to fingerprint me or for me to give them information about my family, and I'd always refused. I didn't think I needed to be fingerprinted because criminals get fingerprinted and I wasn't a criminal. I also didn't like the idea of them having any sort of access to my family, their addresses, or even their names. My parents were both dead, but I still had a brother and a sister and a wife and son, and I didn't want anyone in Pakistan knowing where they lived, because who knows what they might have done with that information?

After the superintendent and the man from the Home Department excused themselves and stepped out of the room, I took the opportunity to speak directly with Carmela. "So what's going on now? Has anything changed since I talked to you last?"

"Not really. We seem to be stuck in a holding pattern ever since the Lahore High Court agreed on Thursday to the Pakistani government's request to delay its ruling on whether or not you have diplomatic immunity. I think we should consider this to be a positive development because the lawyer representing the Punjab government seemed pretty adamant that you did *not* have diplomatic immunity. We're going to be putting this extension to good use. We're working round the clock on this. You just need to hang in there until March 14. That's when your next hearing is, okay?"

"What's that, three more weeks? I can handle that just fine as long I know I'm not being forgotten about. I'm starting to think I may never get out of here."

"Please trust me, Ray. There's a lot going on behind the scenes you don't know about. Discussions are taking place at a very high level. Kerry's visit got the ball rolling. Both sides are talking now. It's just a very complicated issue. There are a lot of moving parts. But I can assure you that we're doing everything in our power to get you out of here."

I nodded. "I understand that diplomatic channels move slowly. But are we applying any pressure on them? Do we have any leverage?"

Carmela nodded to me as the superintendent and the Home Department official returned to the room and reclaimed their seats. "There are several different avenues we're exploring. But if they all turn into dead ends, if the Pakistani government refuses to cooperate with us for some reason," she raised her voice so that everyone in the room could clearly hear her, "we're looking into cutting off all the funds coming into the country from the United States. The next $500 million payment from the Kerry–Lugar–Berman aid package is due, but we're considering withholding it if they don't release you soon."

The superintendent and the Home Department official had been chatting when they'd returned to the room, but upon hearing Carmela's warning, both of them stopped talking. This wasn't an idle threat, and they knew it. The United States had been forced to withhold all or some of its aid packages to Pakistan many times in the past. One of the first instances occurred in 1963, when President Lyndon Johnson withheld a $4.3 million loan meant to upgrade one of Pakistan's airports, after Pakistan announced it would be running commercial airline flights to and from communist China.

More commonly, the United States had withheld aid in an attempt to dissuade Pakistan's nuclear ambitions, which made themselves known publicly for the first time in 1965. After Pakistan and India fought a brief war in the hotly contested Kashmir region, the second of three wars the two countries have fought there, Pakistan's foreign minister, Zulfikar Ali Bhutto, said, "If India builds the [nuclear] bomb, we will eat grass or leaves, even go hungry, but we will get one of our own." His words were almost prophetic. While serving as president from 1971 to 1973 and prime minister from 1973 to 1977, he helped usher Pakistan into the nuclear age, despite his country's inability to produce enough wheat to feed its own people.

From that time forward, US aid to Pakistan became conditional on Pakistan ending its nuclear program. When it was discovered in 1979 that Pakistan was being noncompliant, President Jimmy Carter, in accordance with the Symington Amendment to the Arms Export Control Act, ceased making payments on the $85 million aid package it had promised Pakistan. Adhering to the similarly worded Pressler Amendment, President George H. W. Bush did the same in 1990, halting $570 million in assistance after obtaining evidence that Pakistan had built a nuclear weapon.

While Pakistani leaders had happily turned down US aid in the past in favor of building a nuclear arsenal—Pakistan now has more than 100 nuclear warheads—it was becoming harder and harder for them to do, as the country had grown increasingly dependent on foreign aid and loans from such organizations as the International Monetary Fund and the World Bank. Without this financial support, Pakistan's economy would go into freefall, and everyone knew it.

Carmela's not-so-veiled threat had a noticeable effect on the superintendent and the Home Department official. She'd succeeded in getting their full attention. You could see it on their faces. This was very big news they were being asked to deliver. But they recovered quickly, resuming their conversation about who knows what. While they were talking in Urdu, Carmela handed me a piece of paper.

"Samir asked me to give you this note."

I must have looked confused.

"Just read it," she said.

I did. Samir had written it, he explained in the note, on his way out of the country. After his picture and name had appeared in a local newspaper in conjunction with my case, he'd received several death threats. As he was driving to the consulate a few days earlier, the threats turned real. Two SUVs pulled up alongside him and tried to cut him off. To get away from them, he had to swerve into a McDonald's parking lot, hoping the drop-arm barrier at the entrance would act as a deterrent. His evasive maneuver appeared to have worked. The SUVs drove off. He lingered at the McDonald's long enough to presume he was safe, but as soon as he pulled out of the parking lot, the SUVs appeared in his rearview mirror. They tried to run him off the road several times, and he came close to crashing. He succeeded in making it to the consulate, but now that he'd been targeted he was no longer safe in Pakistan, so he was put on a plane and flown out of the country.

Samir also mentioned how much he'd enjoyed getting to know me and how often he thought about me. His note really meant a lot to me. He basically said everything I wished I could have said to him, only he said it far more eloquently than I ever could have. Samir's words were so heartfelt they actually made me tear up a little.

"You all right?" Carmela asked.

"Yeah, I'm fine. I'm just really going to miss that guy. He was a good dude. A really good dude. If you ever talk to him, please tell him how grateful I was to get this letter and how much it meant to me."

Carmela was usually every bit as reserved as I was, but seeing me cry made her shed a few tears of her own. She gave my arm another one of her sympathetic pats. "I know he would've liked to have been able to say goodbye in person, but, obviously, he couldn't."

I nodded. "I understand."

While we were talking, the superintendent stood up from the table. "Before I go, I must emphasize, once again, how important it is that we be able to fingerprint Mr. Davis."

His timing was just about as bad as it could have possibly been. Carmela bolted upright and shot him a withering look. "No! Do not ask me about fingerprinting him again. Mr. Davis has diplomatic immunity. He should be turned over to the diplomatic mission in Islamabad. End of discussion."

The superintendent froze and nodded his head dumbly. He looked as if he'd been punched in the gut and was waiting for the air to return to his lungs so he could start breathing again. He didn't walk so much as stumble out of the room with the Home Department official at his side.

"And I'm holding you personally accountable for his safety," Carmela shouted at his back. "If anything happens to him while he's here, you're the one who's going to be held responsible for it."

BEFORE CARMELA LEFT, she gave me a hug, something she hadn't done before, and as she did she whispered in my ear. "You don't have to give them your fingerprints. You don't have to give them *anything* if you don't want to. But if they're going to torture you over it, just do it. Don't let them hurt you. It's not worth it."

As nice as it was to get her backing on this, the way she'd stood up to the superintendent impressed me even more. Her boldness made me more determined than ever to take a stand. I knew my rights. I had diplomatic immunity. By not turning me over to the US Embassy, the Pakistanis were violating international law. I didn't have to give them anything. So when two guards came to get me that afternoon, I was inspired to object. When they asked me to stand up, I refused.

"Another interview?" I asked.

"No, we're taking you to get fingerprinted."

"I'm sorry. I'm not doing that. I'm not giving you my fingerprints."

I'd made up my mind. If they wanted to get my fingerprints, they were going to have to break my hands. That's how far I was prepared to go.

I succeeded in getting them to leave. But holding onto this sort of back-to-the wall mentality affects different people in different ways, and mine manifested itself in a way I would never have expected.

I don't normally dream, or at least I never remember it if I do, but I did that night. In the dream, the guards actually break my hands in order to get my fingerprints. I get released from the prison soon afterward. During the plane ride home, both of my hands are in casts, and at one point I hear a bunch of voices shouting at me from behind. "Hey, brother, we're glad you're out! Congratulations, man!"

I turn around and see Sylvester Stallone and Jason Statham.

"*The Expendables?*" I ask.

Stallone leans over and gives me a bear hug. "We're so happy you made it out of there, bro!"

His embrace is so strong it nearly cracks open my casts, and I start screaming, "My hands! My hands!"

I woke up, covered in a sheen of sweat and well aware of the absurdity of what had just taken place: I *never* dream, and then when I finally do, *that's* the dream I have.

23.

KOT LAKHPAT JAIL, LAHORE, PAKISTAN

(February 20, 2011—Day 25)

F YOU'D ASKED ME while I was in prison if I was being tortured, I would have said no. There are gradations of torture, ranging from subtle to extreme, and after going through SERE training I tended to discount the subtle varieties because the extreme ones had formed such a lasting impression on me.

During my SERE training, I was, by any definition of the word, tortured. The instructors sprayed us with water, crammed us into tiny boxes, and smacked us upside the head. They beat the crap out of us. They weren't allowed to take a full swing, which meant they couldn't pull their hands back beyond their shoulders. But even with half swings they could still generate a lot of force. While standing in formation, at attention but a little out of it after getting almost no sleep for days on end, one of them hit me so hard it locked my jaw in place. I couldn't move it. From the wide-eyed expression on his face I could tell how bad the injury must have looked. He dismissed everyone but me and a medic, who popped my jaw back into place.

Originally created to teach American military personnel who'd been captured overseas how to withstand torture, SERE acquired a divisive edge during the War on Terror when some of its methods were reverse-engineered, renamed "enhanced interrogation techniques," and used against detainees who had been captured by the United States and held in various black sites around the world. The controversy surrounding this issue reached its height during the Abu Ghraib scandal of 2004, which saw eleven soldiers get charged with dereliction of duty, maltreatment, and aggravated assault and battery, and again in 2007, when news leaked that Khalid Sheikh Mohammed, the architect of 9/11, had been water-boarded 183 times while being held at a black site. As the American media and public made their indignation known, I couldn't help but be amused because, as rough as the treatment these detainees received was, what I was taught to endure during SERE training was far worse.

Given my background and training, I didn't consider the treatment I received during my time at Kot Lakhpat Jail to be torture. I hadn't been slapped. I hadn't been beaten. I hadn't been put into any stress positions. I hadn't been waterboarded. I hadn't been stripped naked and had cold water poured on me. I hadn't had my head slammed against a wall. I hadn't had chemicals poured on my skin. I hadn't been threatened by attack dogs. I hadn't been forced to wear a diaper. I hadn't been sodomized with a broom handle. *But . . .*

But I had been subject to lengthy interrogation sessions. I had been yelled at. I had been exposed to extreme cold, forced to use nearly frozen water to bathe. I had been ogled nearly every time I took a bath, which would make anyone extremely uncomfortable. I had been deprived of sleep (or at least had my sleep disrupted), thanks to the overhead lights staying on twenty-four hours a day. I had been kept in isolation twenty-two hours a day. I had been forced to put up with random visits from the guards, which prevented me from ever being able to completely relax. I had been hooded (during the drive to Cantonment). I had been forced to listen to loud music (until Carmela asked that the speaker blaring music and sermons during the celebration of Muhammad's birthday be moved). I had been denied access to time (until Carmela's request that I be given a clock was granted). And, because I was fed chicken curry and rice every single day I was in prison and nothing else, it could be argued that I had been the victim of dietary manipulation. Personally, I really didn't consider any of this to be torture, but, according to the legal definition of the word, it was.

I'm a robust person. I know how to take a beating. Depending of course on how long I've been hit and with what, I usually come out just fine. So I really wasn't too concerned about the prison staff or any ISI agents getting physical with me. I also couldn't see them crossing that line. From what the consulate personnel had told me, I understood that the incident and my arrest had become an international news story. There would have been severe repercussions around the world if it was discovered that I was being beaten or tortured. It was bad enough that the Pakistani government had detained and was refusing to release someone who had a diplomatic passport. If they'd beaten me and the press found out, it could have led to a breakdown in diplomatic relations with not only the United States but other countries as well, and Pakistan simply couldn't afford to see its standing in the international community fall any lower.

Adding to my confidence, the next time the consulate personnel visited me, they brought with them the one thing I'd been needing the most ever since the lawyer who'd represented me in court on February 11 abruptly quit: a team of lawyers who promised to stick around.

WHY IT TOOK SO LONG for me to get legal representation says a lot about how much influence terrorist organizations had in Pakistan. As soon as news of the incident reached the DOJ, it was clear that I was going to need its assistance. There was only one DOJ lawyer in all of Pakistan at the time, so by default the responsibility for acquiring legal representation for me fell into his lap.

Peter Strasser was in Pakistan in a training capacity. The assignment he'd been given was to educate and train local prosecutors, no easy task given the state of the Pakistani legal system. Thanks to a host of inadequacies, including impossible caseloads, incompetent police, corrupt judges, and their own inexperience, prosecutors in Pakistan had an abysmally low conviction rate of 26 percent. Up until January 27, Strasser's main function was helping local prosecutors increase that rate. After January 27, his regular duties were suspended, and overseeing my case became his primary responsibility. But as someone who was in charge of training *prosecutors*, it would have reflected poorly on him and the DOJ if he were enlisted to act as my defense attorney, so he reached out to all the lawyers he knew in Pakistan, hoping to hire one of them to defend me.

"It was incredibly difficult," he later explained. "It sounds easy—just go find somebody a lawyer—but there wasn't a lawyer in Lahore who wanted to touch that case because they were all scared that if they did they were going to be killed. And it was a reasonable fear because lawyers in Pakistan get killed. If you advocate for a cause that's unpopular with the fundamentalists and the terrorists, then you die. So it's a realistic fear on their part."

Just how challenging Strasser's task was going to be became clear when the first lawyer he hired, Hassam Qadir, quit after just a few days on the job. Strasser spent the next several weeks trying to find an attorney willing to defend me in court. With the assistance of Zahid Hussein Bukhari, the former prosecutor general of Punjab Province, he interviewed every lawyer he could possibly think of, but the only ones inclined to do it were third- and fourth-tier lawyers, and he wasn't about to hire one of them—not for a case with as high a profile as mine had. He preferred to hire someone from the first or second tier, but each of them told him roughly the same thing: "I don't want to do it, but so-and-so might." And on down the line.

Making the task that much harder, any lawyer from the top two tiers who was even mildly interested always insisted on being part of a three-person panel; nobody wanted to go it alone. Complying with this request, Strasser was finally able to convince a very good defense lawyer, along with two other equally competent attorneys, to represent me the day before one of my initial court appearances. The defense lawyer showed up at a meeting at the consulate and discussed my case with Strasser for an hour, but just as he was about to sign the engagement agreement—his pen was actually hovering over the document—he looked at Strasser with dread in his eyes and said, "I'm sorry. I can't do it."

Part of the problem, I later discovered, was that Strasser was expected to hire local counsel for $20,000 or less, and none of the lawyers he interviewed was willing to risk his life for such a small amount of money. Finally, frustrated and running out of ideas, Strasser went back to the man who'd helped him compose the list of lawyers to approach and asked, "Why don't you just do it?"

"Okay, but it will cost—" and Bukhari named some astronomical figure.

Strasser countered with an offer of $100,000.

"Okay, I'll do it for $100,000, but you're going to have to pay for my life insurance policy."

"I'm sorry," Strasser told him, "but for $100,000 you can buy your own life insurance."

CARMELA HAD BEEN TRYING to get me legal representation for three weeks, and her failure to do so was making her increasingly agitated. So it was hard to tell who was more relieved when I was finally introduced to my new legal team, her or me. She had a big smile on her face when she explained that Bukhari was going to act as my local counsel, while an American from the State Department's Legal Advisers Office named Paul—I never did get his last name—would be assisting him. Even though he was playing second fiddle on this, Paul always took on an outsized role during the meetings.

"I want you to know that I'm here to get you out," he assured me. "I'm not leaving Pakistan until you're free."

"Thanks," I said. "I appreciate it."

"And let me assure you that your case is being taken very seriously." He lowered his voice so that the superintendent of the prison and the official from the Home Department, who were also in the room, couldn't hear. "This is being discussed at the highest level of government."

"Yes, sir," I responded, barely able to conceal my growing cynicism. "*The highest level of government*. Roger that."

"I don't think you understand. I'm talking about the *highest* level of government. The president has spoken your name."

I gave him a halfhearted thumbs-up. "Got it."

He turned to Carmela. "Why doesn't he seem to care?"

"I think he's heard this a lot."

"Is that right?" Paul asked me.

"Yes, sir."

"And knowing that doesn't give you any comfort?"

I shook my head. "Look, if the president really is trying to get me released, then why am I still here? I don't know what's holding up the process, but if he can't do it, no one can, which means I'm probably going to be here a *long* time."

"You're looking at it the wrong way, Ray," Paul said. "The fact that this is taking so long is actually good. We're hoping to drag this out. We're going to be filing motions and doing whatever else we can to delay this thing. And some of these motions are very strong. Through his sources, Mr. Bukhari discovered that the two guys you shot had been arrested something like fifty times for doing exactly what you described, holding up people at crowded intersections. Also, when the police searched the bodies, they found some cell phones and credit cards these guys had stolen from other motorists that same day. These two facts are exculpatory, but neither of them were in the *challan* that was submitted by the police. There's also a lot going on behind the scenes you don't know about. High-level talks about ways to get you out of here."

I nodded to show Paul I understood. The knowledge that I now had a team of lawyers to defend me encouraged me to have a little fun at the expense of the superintendent and the Home Department official. For several days, while idling in my cell, I'd been contemplating the pros and cons of a gambit I'd devised, unsure if the benefit I might gain outweighed the potential backlash. But with a team of lawyers at my side, any hesitancy I once felt disappeared.

"Hey, Carmela," I said loud enough for everyone in the room to hear, "do you happen to know who Aafia Siddiqui is?"

I could tell by the expression on her face that she was a little surprised to hear me bring up the name of a convicted terrorist, particularly one who was so popular in Pakistan.

She said "Yes" so hesitantly it sounded more like a question than an answer.

Everyone in the room stopped talking and focused their attention on me. Some of them were actually leaning forward, literally on the edge of their seats.

"Well, as you must know, Aafia Siddiqui is in prison in the United States, and I was told that if I helped secure her release it would go a long way toward getting me out of here. From the way it was explained to me, as soon as she gets released, I would be released. It sounds like I could be out of here in a couple of days. Is this something that's being talked about?"

"Yes, I believe it has been discussed."

I paused and looked around the room, making sure that everyone—particularly the superintendent and the Home Department official—could hear me. "Well, let me just say this: Don't you fucking do it! Do not let them release a convicted terrorist just to get me out of here. I have big shoulders. I can bear this burden. I did nothing wrong. Do you hear me?"

Carmela flashed a hint of a smile. "I understand. I'll make sure the appropriate parties receive that message."

As the prison superintendent and the Home Department official realized that the plan they'd tried to broker via the prison doctor had been shot down, they appeared visibly deflated like a couple of balloons with very small holes in them.

24.

HIGHLANDS RANCH, COLORADO
(February 20, 2011—Day 25)

S O MUCH TIME HAD PASSED *since Ray had been arrested, I was begin-ning to fear the worst—that he might never come home. Although to be perfectly honest, the "worst" and the norm were almost the same. By that point in our marriage, Ray was home so little it was hard to say if we even had a romantic relationship at all. We'd become more like business partners, helping each other as much as we could but doing it more out of duty and mutually assured contentment than love or passion. Even when he was home, it was like he wasn't really there. He was home* physically. *His body was there. But his mind always seemed to be somewhere else.*

I barely saw him in the weeks leading up to his final deployment to Paki-stan. My dad was dying of liver cancer, and I left Ray in charge of our son for a week, so my sisters and I could get my dad into a hospice and clean out his apartment and say goodbye to him. I returned home on a Sunday, and Ray left for Pakistan the very next day.

While Ray was detained, his supervisor Ron called me nearly every single day to give me reports about what was going on. Because of his position in the company—upper-level management—Ron must have been a very busy guy, and yet he'd always take the time to chat with me. He took what felt like a genu-ine interest in my life and was always very sweet. He'd remember to ask how my son was doing. He'd ask how my day had gone. He'd tell me to let him know if I needed anything and was great at giving me some much-needed emotional support. He even called me on Valentine's Day and, three weeks later, on Ray's and my anniversary. We talked about anything and everything. Sometimes we'd be on the phone more than an hour.

The news Ron had to share about Ray usually fell on the spectrum somewhere between good and great. They were working on it, he'd say. They had a plan. But it was a long process. It could take time. But don't despair. It will happen. He rarely got into specifics, and I understood why. I'd gotten used to being in the dark as far as what sort of work Ray did exactly. Ray protected people who were working to preserve American interests overseas, and I really didn't need to know any more than that, did I?

It was an extremely stressful time. Ray's arrest wasn't just nerve-racking for me. It affected everyone he was close to, particularly his sister and brother. They were really torn up about it, but I couldn't allow myself to join them. I had my son to think about. If I fell to pieces, who was going to take care of him? I had to stay strong because there were so many people depending on me. I had no choice but to hold it together. I refused to let myself adopt a defeatist mentality. I decided early on in the crisis that I would just concentrate on taking care of everybody else and not worry about the things I couldn't control.

Adopting this mindset worked, but only up to a point. There were a couple moments when it suddenly became too much, and I broke down. Ray's mom died in 2010, many years after Ray's dad had passed away. My mom died in 2007, and my dad died just three days before Ray was arrested in Pakistan. That my son didn't have any grandparents was bad enough. The idea that he might grow up without a dad? That practically killed me. One night about a week after Ray got arrested was particularly bad. I rocked my son in my arms for a really long time with tears streaming down my face, then called my sister and cried some more. I had to force myself to pull it together. That was the low point for me. After that night, I banished all negative thoughts about Ray's situation from my head. I had to stay positive. If not for me, then for everyone else. Too many people were counting on me. I couldn't fall apart.

As hard as it was to get through each day while Ray was in prison, the media made it so much worse, especially the local outlets. They were relentless. They didn't know when to say when. They set up shop directly in front of our house. They camped out at my son's school. They emailed. They called. They texted. And it never stopped. This went on day after day, hour after hour, every single day. It wasn't unusual for someone to knock on our door just as my son and I were sitting down to eat or as I was giving him a bath or while I was trying to take a nap. They'd ask for an interview, a comment, just two seconds of my time.

The entire time Ray was detained, I responded to every request, answered every phone call, and replied to every email. But the more I gave, the more they wanted. I understood that they were just trying to do their jobs, but they didn't have to do it so aggressively. It got so that I couldn't walk from my car to my house without them descending on me like vultures. I'd say, "No comment, no comment, no comment," and they'd still knock on the door and ask me to say something about Ray's situation. That experience changed my perception of the media, and not for the better.

When I relayed my concerns to Ray's colleague TK, he handed me a business card and said, "If it ever gets to be too much for you, if the media just won't leave you alone, show them this card and tell them to call the number on it and the person on the other end of the line will take care of it for you."

At first, I had no intention of using the card. I put it on my desk and forgot all about it. Still, I appreciated the gesture. I'd come to expect nothing less from these guys. Like Ray, they were doers. They got stuff done. Even if it was just little stuff. They walked the dog around the block for me. They shoveled snow. They vacuumed the house. I'd gotten really sick due to all the stress and anxiety and sleep deprivation I was suffering from, and they were a huge help.

But, to be honest, they added to my stress as much as they relieved it. Don't get me wrong. I enjoyed getting to know them and I was grateful for their company, but in the end their presence was just one more thing I had to worry about. They were guests in my home, and the way I was raised, you take care of your guests. I wanted to be more hospitable toward them, but I was so sleep deprived I didn't know which end was up. I was so overwhelmed at that point in my life I simply didn't have the energy to look after anyone else. And, frankly, I didn't even know why they were there. I even asked Ron if he could send them home. I wasn't used to having help, so it took a while for me to get used to having them around.

But I never got used to the media. They just kept coming at me and coming at me and coming at me. Reporters, cameramen, photographers, all trying to ask me a question, photograph me, film me. Sometimes all at once. Finally, I'd had enough. They were annoying and invasive and disrespectful, and I didn't have anything more to tell them beyond what I'd already said, which was basically, "I don't know anything." After getting more than 100 phone calls in a single week, I remembered the card TK had given me and decided it was time to use it. Something in my gut told me I shouldn't do it, but I went ahead and did it anyway. My logic was simple: I didn't have the time, energy, or finesse to handle all the calls and requests that were coming in every day, so if I could get a little help, why not take advantage of it?

I don't even remember exactly who I gave it to. I think it was someone from 9NEWS, a television station in Denver, but it could have just as easily been someone from ABC or The Today Show. *All of them were there at some point or another.*

"I'm sorry," I told the reporter. "I can't do this right now. But here. Take this. They'll answer all your questions."

25.

KOT LAKHPAT JAIL, LAHORE, PAKISTAN
(February 20, 2011—Day 25)

T HAT I WAS A CIA AGENT was just one of many lies the media spread about me. The Pakistani media were particularly egregious offenders. They printed all kinds of crazy stories about what I was doing in Pakistan. They said that I had my own Afghan army, that I worked with the Taliban to undermine the Pakistani government, that I was the CIA station chief in Islamabad, that I was personally hunting down Osama bin Laden. And on and on. Crazy, outlandish stuff that made my family and friends back home scratch their heads and say, "What in the world has Ray been up to?"

The "news" that I was a spy was especially hard for Rebecca because she had to deal with the fallout. When people hear an exciting but false story and a boring but true one, they're usually going to be far more interested in spreading the lie. The uproar that ensued wasn't Rebecca's fault, but she still felt bad about it for a very long time and still does to this day.

Word of the scandal reached me via the consulate personnel. The next time they visited, Dale pulled me aside and whispered in my ear, "It's all over the media. They think you're a CIA agent."

"Well," I said, trying to look at the bright side, "at least they're not questioning me anymore."

26.

MUSCAT, OMAN
(February 23, 2011—Day 28)

A S OFTEN AS I WAS TOLD that getting me out was a top priority for the US government, I had no idea what was actually going on behind the scenes. Very few people did. In its efforts to get me released, the US government had adopted a two-pronged approach, one that was highly visible and one that was far less so. "You could describe it as above the waterline and below the waterline," Ambassador Munter said years afterward. "Above the waterline, we were protesting, saying they had no right to take Ray to court. And below the waterline, we were initiating the talks to try to get him freed."

No two characters in this unfolding drama worked farther below the waterline than CIA director Leon Panetta and ISI's director-general, Ahmed Shuja Pasha. Panetta was a longtime Washington insider. He represented California's 16th Congressional District from 1977 to 1993 and was President Bill Clinton's chief of staff from 1994 to 1997. Despite Panetta's wealth of experience inside the Beltway, President Obama's decision to appoint him head of the CIA in January 2009 was a bit of a surprise, as Panetta, having served in the army for just two years in the 1960s, had very little experience in the military and intelligence communities.

In that regard, Panetta's ISI counterpart, General Pasha, was nearly his opposite. Pasha began serving in the Pakistan Army in 1974 and climbed all the way up the military's ladder, getting named director general of military operations in 2006. Two years later, Pakistan's army chief, General Kayani, tapped Pasha to be the next leader of ISI. Just two months after Pasha's appointment, a three-day-long killing spree left 164 people dead in Mumbai, India, an attack he was accused of orchestrating in a November 2010 lawsuit.

As much tension as there'd been between the CIA and ISI over the years, my situation escalated it to an even higher level. I would later find out that shortly before John Kerry's February 15 visit to Pakistan, General Pasha had flown to Washington and asked Panetta point-blank if I worked for the CIA. Panetta responded that I didn't and that the State Department, not the CIA, was handling the matter.

Pasha was angered by Panetta's response and grew even more so when Ambassador Munter, after clearing it with officials from the White House and State Department, explained to him the exact nature of my job. Pasha understood how important it was—for both sides—to get me out of Pakistan as soon as possible, but like his country's president and prime minister he was happy to let me remain in jail until an acceptable solution to this increasingly vexing problem could be found.

Working on the problem from the opposite side of the table, Panetta sat down with Pakistan's ambassador to the United States, Husain Haqqani, on February 21 and asked for his assistance in getting me out of jail. Haqqani was largely viewed as being pro-American, but in this instance he wasn't so accommodating.

Two days later, the top military brass for both countries met at a luxury beach resort in Oman on the eastern tip of the Arabian Peninsula. The top-secret meeting had been scheduled months before my arrest to discuss the war in Afghanistan, but my situation ended up consuming a large portion of it. Both sides left saying all the right things.

"I was very grateful for General Kayani's time and the opportunity to continue the dialogue and the relationship at this very critical time in the effort," Admiral Mike Mullen, chairman of the Joint Chiefs of Staff, said to reporters.

"I was pleased to have the opportunity to discuss with American officers the progress we have made fighting extremists in our country and to offer them my thoughts about how our two sides might better cooperate," General Kayani responded in the press.

An unidentified "senior Pakistani official" offered a far more substantive take on the meeting to the *Cable*, *Foreign Policy* magazine's online branch: "The idea is to find a solution whereby the Davis incident does not hijack the US–Pakistan relationship. The relationship remains testy, but after the meeting between Mullen and Kayani the likelihood of some resolution has increased."

WHILE PROGRESS WAS BEING MADE to resolve my case, for many it wasn't being made fast enough. The longer my situation dragged on, the more irritated people got, and as the point man on the diplomatic side of the operation, Ambassador Munter bore the brunt of much of that frustration.

"During that period a lot of people in Washington sent me messages saying, 'These guys [General Pasha and General Kayani] are taking you for a ride. What are you really doing to get [Raymond Davis] out? What are we going to do?' and I would say, 'We have to be patient. We have to work with them. We don't really have much of a choice.' Well, a lot of people were very concerned that that wouldn't work."

The need for the US government to get me out sooner rather than later was growing increasingly urgent, and the reason was even more secretive than the meeting in Oman had been. In June 2010, after nearly a decade of searching for bin Laden without success, the CIA picked up some valuable intel about Abu Ahmed al-Kuwaiti, aka Ibrahim Saeed Ahmed, who was believed to be bin Laden's personal courier. It was the agency's most promising lead in the hunt for bin Laden since 2001, when he'd escaped from Tora Bora, the complex of caves in Afghanistan's White Mountains he used as a hideout, and fled into Pakistan.

Two months after the discovery, CIA agents followed Ahmed to a sprawling compound in the upper-middle-class neighborhood of Bilal Town in Abbottabad, a "hill station," or resort town, in the verdant Orash Valley roughly forty miles north of Islamabad. The compound stuck out due to the lengths it went to remain obscure. The walls on its southern side were so tall that it was impossible for passersby to see into the courtyard. The windows on the second and third floors of the main building had been blacked out to prevent anyone from seeing in or out. The occupants burned their trash. And, perhaps most shocking in this day and age, the compound didn't have a telephone or Internet connection. Whoever was living there had cut off all ties with the outside world, and the CIA, after months of observation, believed there was a very good chance that it was bin Laden and his family who were holed up inside.

In December 2010, Leon Panetta met with President Obama to present the intelligence that led him to believe that it was more likely than not that bin Laden was hiding in the compound. The president asked him to start working on a plan to capture or kill the terrorist, and to that end Panetta started hosting regular meetings with Admiral William McRaven at the CIA's headquarters in Langley, Virginia. By late February 2011, while I was stuck in Lahore's Kot Lakhpat Jail, Panetta and McRaven had made a list of the three best ways to raid the compound and take out bin Laden. The first was to destroy the entire compound and any tunnels that might be underneath it with bombs dropped from a B-2 stealth bomber. The second was to drop an SF team directly into the compound using helicopters. The third was to reach out to the Pakistani government, giving it an opportunity to assist with the operation.

The last option was never seriously considered. As Panetta explained in an interview with Peter Mansbridge of the CBC network the following year, "The concern we had is that, you know, we had provided intelligence to them with regards to other areas and unfortunately, for one way or another, it got leaked to the individuals we were trying to go after. So as a result of that we were concerned that if we were going to perform a sensitive mission like this, we had to do it on our own."

Defense Secretary Robert Gates initially came out in support of the first option. His reasoning was that using American military forces inside Pakistan would be a violation of that nation's sovereignty. He was quickly overruled by Obama, who, as much as he wanted to see bin Laden taken out, also wanted proof of his death. Bunker-busting bombs dropped from 30,000 feet wouldn't leave much in the way of DNA.

Which left the second option. By late February the president was close to signing off on a plan to send an SF team into Pakistan to raid the compound in Abbottabad, but a bunch of logistical details needed to be sorted out before it could be set in motion. I was one of those details. A concern circulating around Washington was that if I wasn't released before the raid on the compound, the Pakistanis, angry that they hadn't been consulted, might retaliate by killing me. Those in Pakistan responsible for my welfare needed to get me out of the country first, and they needed to do it fast before bin Laden could slip away once again.

27.

KOT LAKHPAT JAIL, LAHORE, PAKISTAN
(March 3, 2011—Day 36)

A FTER BEING INCARCERATED for five long weeks, I was starting to lose hope. Any cockiness I'd once had—"Fourteen days is easy!"—had begun to fade to a dull despair. Every day seemed the same. Eat some chicken curry and rice. Get in a workout. Read a book. And hope this wasn't the day the consulate personnel stopped showing up. Their visits were like a lifeline, helping me to stay afloat. But they could only do so much, and they knew it, so one day they brought in Herb to talk to me.

Herb was an American psychologist stationed in India. He was an older man—seventy, maybe even eighty years old—but he was in incredible shape. He moved around like someone half his age. Herb and I hit it off right away because he actually knew someone from my past. One of the first things he said to me was, "Your friend J. J. from high school asked me to say hi. Do you know who I'm talking about?"

"I know exactly who you're talking about!"

J. J. and I had graduated from high school at the same time and had followed very similar career paths. Around the time I joined the army, he became an Air Force pilot, flying F-16 jets. We were just a couple of good ol' boys from Big Stone Gap, Virginia, but each of us ended up seeing more of the world than the entire population of our hometown put together. Even more amazing is that, despite serving in different branches of the military, we always seemed to get stationed near each other. Both of us were in Iraq at about the same time. And Tucson, Arizona. And Las Vegas. So it didn't surprise me nearly as much as it probably should have to hear that J. J. was stationed in India at the same time I was working in Pakistan. It was almost as if we were following each other around the world. Funny how something so small—Herb knowing an old friend of mine—could carry so much weight, but it did. I felt comfortable in his presence almost immediately.

"You seem to be handling this situation very well," he said.

I shrugged.

"How are you doing physically?"

"I'm holding up all right. Every day I do pushups, squats, whatever I can think of."

"How about yoga? You ever do that?"

I shook my head.

"I'd love to show you some poses. I think it would really help you."

"You know, I think I've got the physical part covered, Herb. I should be good there."

He held my gaze about a second longer than most people would have, as if trying to ascertain whether I was telling the truth. "What about meditation? Ever tried that?"

"Yeah, a couple times actually. I think it was guided mediation. It helped me relax. But I don't know enough about it to do it myself."

"Well, I can help you with that. I can to teach you how to guide yourself, so in the future you won't need any assistance from anyone else. Sound good?"

I nodded. "Sure."

"Okay, when you go back to your cell, I want you to find a relaxing position to be in for a while. You can sit on the floor or on a chair or you can lie on your bed. Whatever feels the most comfortable. Then close your eyes and picture yourself opening the door to your cell and slowly walking down the hall. It doesn't matter where you're going. What's important is that you're leaving your cell behind you.

"There's a door at the end of the hallway. You open it, and you see a set of stairs leading down. Start walking down the stairs. Take your time. Each step you take relaxes your mind a little bit more, and by the time you reach the bottom you're in a completely new environment. Some place that you know and find calming. The mountains, the beach, a park in the middle of a city. Anywhere that makes you feel at ease. Listen to the sounds of this new environment: a breeze coming off the ocean, a waterfall cascading down a creek, children laughing. Smell the fresh air. Enjoy the serenity. Stay here as long as you like."

Herb stopped talking. A minute passed, maybe two.

"When you're ready," he continued in the same quiet but assured voice, "slowly walk back up the steps and close the door behind you. Then walk back down the hallway to your cell and close that door behind you. Take a deep breath and open your eyes. You're back in your cell right where you started, but now you know that you can leave it anytime you want. Doing this exercise is going to be really good for you mentally. It's going to give your mind the release it needs."

I was a bit skeptical, but Herb was a really nice guy, so I told him, "Okay, I'll give it a shot."

And I did. The first couple times Herb visited me I let him guide me, but before long I was doing it all by myself, and I was amazed at the results. Doing this simple exercise allowed me to escape from my reality without requiring the assistance of anyone else. While my body remained trapped inside my jail cell, I knew I could mentally leave it whenever I wanted. It became such a comfort to me that I would actually catch myself meditating while I was engaged in some other activity. I would be lying on my thin mattress on the concrete floor in my cell, but in my mind I would be lying on my bed in our house in Colorado. Physically, I'd be doing a workout in my cell, but, mentally, I'd be at the gym at home. When I sat down at the rickety table in my cell to choke down some chicken curry and rice, I'd imagine I was actually eating a fat steak with crispy fries. While reading a book, sometimes I'd actually forget where I was, tricked for a moment into thinking I was at home on the couch. In this way, I meditated for hours and hours every day. Even though I was stuck inside a prison cell, I guess you could say I was enjoying a mini-vacation inside my head.

I thought I had a pretty strong mind before the incident in Pakistan occurred, but learning how to do guided meditation amplified it exponentially. And the benefits didn't just come as I was doing it. Its positive effects often carried over to the rest of my day. I started to feel more relaxed, better rested, calmer.

Which was a good and necessary thing because, as relieved as I was to finally have legal representation, the news my attorneys shared with me was rarely good. The attorney Peter Strasser had convinced to represent me, Zahid Hussein Bukhari, stuck to a plan that had been devised in high-level meetings and had trickled its way down the ranks, and that was to delay proceedings for as long as possible in order to give those working behind the scenes more time to work out a settlement. Bukhari would come up with various ways to accomplish this goal and pass his ideas along to Strasser, who would then run them through the proper channels in DC. Once these ideas were approved—and they always were—Bukhari would draft a motion, Strasser would edit it, then Bukhari would file it. As long as we kept filing preliminary motions, the charges against me couldn't be framed. My legal team filed six motions in all, including one about Faizan Haider and Muhammad Faheem's lengthy arrest records and one about the stolen property that was recovered from their bodies. Under normal circumstances, the judge, after hearing such exculpatory evidence, would have thrown out the *challan* and made the police start their investigation all over again, but my case was anything but normal. All six motions were denied.

It was clear from this and the fact that the two men I'd shot had never been convicted a single time (even though they'd been arrested more than fifty times!) that they must have been connected to a very powerful person. Yes, the conviction rate in Pakistan is abysmally low, but that doesn't explain this anomaly. With so many arrests on their record, the two of them should have been in jail awaiting trial—at the very least. To get fifty-something charges dismissed, they had to be friends with someone who was extremely wealthy, very well connected politically, or affiliated with ISI. In Pakistan, those are the only three viable choices in a situation like this, which might explain how the rumor that the two men were ISI agents got started.

The many preliminary hearings I went to didn't go so well, either. At a Sessions Court hearing set up inside the prison on March 3, Bukhari, in his first official appearance on my behalf, argued that I could not be prosecuted by that court because the issue of whether or not I had diplomatic immunity had yet to be decided by the Lahore High Court. After a great deal of debate between the prosecution and the defense, the judge rejected my claim for immunity, declaring that neither I nor the Pakistani government had produced any documents proving I had that status.

If there was any good news to come out of that appearance, it was that I still had yet to be formally charged with a crime. I have Bukhari to thank for this, as his plea, that he hadn't received all the documents related to my case, was accepted by the judge. The judge also extended my judicial remand until March 15 and adjourned my case until March 8, at which time the missing documents were to be given to my legal team.

Many in the press believed I would also be indicted that day, but during that hearing Bukhari worked his magic once again, insisting that I couldn't be charged until he'd received all the *complete* documents related to my case. This technicality bought me a little more time, but not much. The judge let it be known that, barring some major disaster, the charges against me would be framed in eight days and the case would proceed directly to trial.

"[Raymond Davis] is probably going to be charged with murder at the next hearing, which is on March 16," Bukhari told the media afterward.

I had only one real chance left of getting out of this mess. I was scheduled to attend a hearing before the Lahore High Court on March 14, at which time the federal government would determine, once and for all, whether I had diplomatic immunity or not. If it was decided that I did, I would be released. But I knew the chances of that actually happening were slim. With tensions in the country still running high, with protests still taking place in all the major cities, and with religious extremists issuing threats against me, any judge who ruled that I had diplomatic immunity and allowed me to go free would probably be killed before the day was over.

It didn't help my cause that the Pakistani newspapers continued to spread outrageous lies about me. One article claimed that the assistant superintendent had smuggled "spy gadgetry" into my cell: a flash drive, a portable hard drive, memory cards—you know, standard computer components. This never happened. Another said that some of my family members had flown into Islamabad and were staying in a guest house there. This also never happened. Another maintained that the police had arrested forty-five people who had been "in constant contact" with me. This might have been partially true. I imagine the police really did arrest those poor people, but did I know all of them? No. According to the article, the police had obtained this information from my cell phone, but, if you recall, that phone really didn't belong to me. It was used by whoever was doing my job and would get passed from one contractor to the next. For all I knew, the police had rounded up a bunch of people who'd been friends with the guy I'd replaced and thrown them all in jail.

The battles being fought in the media every day reflected the growing desperation of all parties involved. I'd become a pawn in a game that was much bigger than myself. For ISI, I was leverage that could be used in negotiations with the US government. For the many religious radicals in the country, I was a glaring example of that perceived overreach as well as an excellent excuse to protest in the streets and set various objects on fire. For the Pakistani government, I was an extremely complicated problem. Allowing me to go free would make it look as if it were kowtowing to American interests and would alienate a majority of the population, but at the same time refusing to do so would jeopardize its long-standing relationship with the United States. For the US government, I posed an equally complex challenge because, once it assumed responsibility for me, getting me out of jail had become one of its top foreign policy objectives, and failing to do so might have wrecked the mission to take out Osama bin Laden or even have destroyed its alliance with Pakistan.

With the interests of so many different groups at stake, pleasing all of them and getting me out of jail seemed to be incompatible ideas. Those working behind the scenes to get me released needed to find a solution that satisfied all sides. I had to be exonerated of all charges and allowed to leave the country, but the Pakistani government couldn't be made to look weak, and the American government couldn't appear as if it had dictated the terms of the deal.

There had to be a way to satisfy all these requirements, but no one I'd spoken to ever seemed to know what that might be.

28.

KOT LAKHPAT JAIL, LAHORE, PAKISTAN
(March 14, 2011—Day 47)

F OR A COUNTRY OFFICIALLY named the Islamic Republic of Pakistan, religion played a surprisingly small role in governmental affairs during its infancy. Mohammad Ali Jinnah, Pakistan's founder and first governor-general, dedicated his life to helping Muslims from the British Indian Empire get their very own state, but, in keeping with his secular personality, the brand of Islam he championed was actually quite moderate.

Jinnah wore hand-tailored suits and silk ties. He drove imported cars. He never wore a beard. He drank whiskey. He mainly spoke English. He married a non-Muslim. And he viewed Islam more as a unifying element of the fledging nation's national identity and a source of culture and philosophy than a foundation upon which to build its government and legal system. When asked by Pakistan's first defense secretary, Major General Iskander Ali Mirza, if he was going to make Pakistan an Islamic nation, Jinnah reportedly replied, "Nonsense! I'm going to have a *modern* state."

This sort of broad-minded liberalism lived on even after Jinnah's death in 1948. The Koran forbids Muslims from consuming alcohol, but that didn't stop one of Pakistan's founding fathers, Prime Minister Liaquat Ali Khan, from downing so many drinks during a May 3, 1950, visit to Washington that Assistant Secretary of State George McGhee came away talking about how impressed he was by the man's tolerance.

A small but vocal percentage of the Pakistani population lobbied for less separation of church and state during the nation's early years, but their wish wasn't granted until General Muhammad Zia-ul-Haq came to power in the 1970s. Prime Minister Zulfikar Ali Bhutto made Zia a lieutenant general in 1975, and the following year he promoted the thirty-year military veteran to army chief. Bhutto was apparently under the impression that Zia would be easy to control, but in that assumption he'd made a fatal error. Zia staged a coup that deposed Bhutto, and, after a sham trial, had him sentenced to death. After assuming control of the country via martial law, Zia made "Islamization," aka "Shariazation"—the process of turning a society into a theocracy, with a strict interpretation of Islam at the forefront—the centerpiece of his administrative rule.

During his eleven-year reign, Zia succeeded in changing life in Pakistan from the ground up. He used government funds to build thousands of *madrassas*, religious schools that teach an austere form of Islam and often promote jihad. Books that were considered un-Islamic were heavily edited or removed from libraries. Western culture was vilified. The national television network PTV replaced music videos with patriotic songs. Theaters that showed Western films were shut down. Women were ordered to cover their heads while in public, restricted from attending school or playing sports, and saw their value in the eyes of the law literally reduced to a fraction of a man's. And every Muslim adult was required to pay *zakat*, giving a small percentage of his wealth to his community's poor each year.

One of the most sweeping and controversial changes Zia made was overhauling the Pakistani legal system. In 1979, he replaced parts of the Pakistani Penal Code with the *Hudood* Ordinances, which promoted Sharia law and instituted punishments lifted straight out of the Koran. An unmarried person caught having extramarital sex could now be given a hundred lashes, while a married one could be stoned to death. Thieves faced the prospect of having their right hands amputated.

To ensure that these draconian measures were actually enforced, Zia created the Federal Shariat Court and the Shariat Appellate Bench of the Supreme Court and empowered them to decide cases based on the teachings of the Koran. Overseen exclusively by Muslim judges, these courts could review any existing law for its conformity with the injunctions of Islam and invalidate those that didn't pass muster. Technically, the Federal Shariat Court fell under the jurisdiction of Pakistan's Supreme Court, but in reality it amounted to an entirely separate judicial system.

Despite Zia's apparent religious zeal, there's evidence to suggest that his reasons for promoting Shariazation were more political in nature. In 1979, when the Shariat bench of the Peshawar High Court, which Zia himself had created, ordered his government to amend Pakistan's secular murder laws to bring them more in line with the injunctions of Islam, Zia appealed the decision. When the Shariat Appellate Bench of the Supreme Court issued the same ruling the following year, Zia shot it down once again. It wasn't until two years after Zia's death that the secular murder laws were finally modified and the *Qisas and Diyat* Ordinance, which required murders to be tried under Sharia law, was adopted. The ordinance was re-promulgated—in Pakistan, ordinances only last four months at a time—more than twenty times before it finally became an Act of Parliament in 1997. From an American's perspective such caution seems wise, as the new ordinance replaced nearly forty sections of the Pakistan Penal Code, completely overhauling the nation's laws related to serious physical injuries and murder.

Zia's dictatorship came to an abrupt end on August 17, 1988, when his plane crashed in a remote desert of Pakistan, but his influence lived on in the Sharia court system he created and the many *madrassa*-educated children who grew up to be religious radicals. One of them was Nek Mohammed, a charismatic Pashtun militant whose death created a vacuum eagerly filled by the leaders of the various tribal militias living in the FATA. On December 12, 2007, some forty of these men convened in North Waziristan and, under the leadership of Baitullah Mehsud, formed the Pakistani Taliban (TTP). In contrast with the Afghan Taliban, which was covertly supported by the Pakistani government via ISI, the TTP considered the Pakistani government to be the enemy. The organization's ultimate goal was to overthrow the state and replace it with one that enforced Sharia law. Its more immediate objective was to push the Pakistani military out of the tribal areas.

By 2008, the TTP had succeeded in establishing a foothold in Swat, a picturesque valley ninety miles north of Islamabad. That year, 3,000 Taliban managed to drive 12,000 Pakistani soldiers out of the valley, destroy more than a hundred girls' schools, and force more than 100,000 people to flee their homes. In February 2009, President Zardari agreed to a ceasefire between the Pakistani military and the TTP in Swat. Instead of driving the TTP out of the valley, Zardari's government tried to appease them, and the Taliban responded by breaking the ceasefire, gaining control of even more territory, and implementing their strict and unforgiving interpretation of Sharia law.

Throughout the Swat region, the Taliban forced men to grow beards longer than a fist, placed *Shaving Is Banned* signs in local barber shops, and torched any businesses that ignored the edict. They ordered women to more or less disappear, insisting they cover their faces and bodies when going out in public and forcing those who worked in government offices to quit. They destroyed stores that sold Western entertainment. They banned the sorts of things (marbles, cigarettes, toothpaste) and activities (dancing, singing, watching television) that made even the hardest lives somewhat bearable. And they executed anyone who stood up to them, including the police.

Foremost among those who were unwilling to stand up to the TTP was President Zardari, who, two months after the failed ceasefire in Swat, signed a bill officially making Sharia the law of the land there. Zardari had shown the same sort of weakness while I was imprisoned in Kot Lakhpat Jail. Instead of taking an active role and helping to resolve the matter, he'd continually shirked his duty, happy to let others decide my fate. But he could only avoid getting involved for so long. On March 14, the government was supposed to rule, one way or another, whether I had diplomatic immunity or not. How Zardari ruled would effectively decide whether I lived or died. The onus was on him, but, given his track record, I shouldn't have been all that surprised when at the very last second he managed to avoid taking a stand and passed the burden along to the courts.

Joining Zardari in his refusal to rule on my status was Chief Justice of the Lahore High Court Ijaz Ahmed Chaudhry, the same judge who'd put me on the Exit Control List six weeks earlier. During the hearing, lawyers from Pakistan's Foreign Office confirmed that I had a diplomatic passport as well as a visa, but Chaudhry declined to rule on whether I had diplomatic immunity, instead proclaiming that that decision should be made by the Sessions Court since it was already hearing my criminal trial.

"The High Court punted," Peter Strasser explained years later. "It was a hot potato. Nobody wanted to be associated with that case."

For me, this was very bad news. The clock that my legal team had been working so hard to slow down had suddenly sped up. In two days, I was going to be tried for murder.

29.

KOT LAKHPAT JAIL, LAHORE, PAKISTAN
(March 16, 2011—Day 49)

I DIDN'T SLEEP VERY MUCH the night before my next court date. This was the big one. After all the hearings and motions and delays, I'd been told that there was no longer any way to drag this thing out. I was, in all likelihood, going to be charged with murder and put on trial the following day. It was nerve-racking, to say the least. My only consolation was the fact that I'd been told the night before that I'd be able to meet with my legal team first thing in the morning and that it would be there to guide me through the next phase of this ordeal.

At 7 A.M., a guard entered my cell and told me that I needed to get ready for court. He also brought me some hot water and two Starbucks Via instant coffee packets. The consulate personnel had given me the coffee, but I wasn't allowed to drink it whenever I wanted to or even keep it in my cell. The prison staff was in charge of dispensing it to me, and they didn't let me drink coffee every morning, only on days I went to court. This must have been a special day because I wasn't forced to make do with a single packet of coffee and no cream as usual. The guard actually gave me *two* packets and some French vanilla creamer as well.

I took a sip and said, "It's going to be a good day, Tater." If you're unfamiliar with Ron White's comedy act, specifically the sketch where he stuffs his bulldog's jowls with M&Ms while the dog's sleeping, that line will mean nothing to you. If you are familiar with it, you should be laughing right now, because how could you not? I always do.

As I was drinking my coffee, I expected my lawyers to show up at any moment, but, glancing at my clock, I saw that it was now 8 A.M. and none of them had arrived yet.

I made another cup, and before I knew it, it was 9 A.M.

Still no lawyers.

10 A.M.

Nothing.

By the time 11 A.M. rolled around, I had a pretty good idea what was going on. The prison staff were back to their old tricks, playing their little mind games with me. I expected them to come to my cell and say, "We're sorry, but you don't have enough time to talk with your attorney anymore. You need to go straight to court."

It was past 11 A.M. by the time the guard who'd told me to get ready hours earlier finally returned to my cell and said, "Let's go. You're late."

Despite how nervous I was about the impending trial, the double dose of coffee had me feeling pretty good. I grinned at the guard. "How can I be late? I've been up since 7 A.M.!"

The guard didn't think that was very funny. He glared at me before leading me to the courtyard outside, where another guard approached me with a pair of handcuffs. When the new guard went to put the cuffs on me, I waved my hand in front of his face like Obi-Wan Kenobi in the "These aren't the droids you're looking for" scene in *Star Wars* and said, "You don't need those handcuffs." And it almost worked! The guard got this really funny look on his face and turned to his boss and asked him something in Urdu. I imagined he said something like, "We don't need to use these?" because his boss started berating him. "Put the handcuffs on him. Put them on now. We need to go."

The now frazzled guard placed one end of the handcuffs on me and the other on himself, but he didn't take me directly into the courtroom. Instead he led me into a small room off to the side, where I was greeted by Carmela, my team of lawyers, and the superintendent of the prison. I took a seat and nodded at the guard to whom I was attached.

"I was told I was going to have attorney-client privilege," I said. "I'm not talking in front of this guy."

"I'm sorry," the superintendent said to my legal team, "but Mr. Davis is a deceptive and dangerous individual and must remain handcuffed at all times."

Bukhari argued in Urdu that there was no way for me to escape, since there was only one window in the room and it had bars on it. The superintendent eventually relented. The guard removed my handcuffs, and the superintendent and the guard left the room.

"So what's the plan for today?" I asked.

The lawyers representing me told me they planned to keep doing exactly what they'd been doing up to this point, dragging out the proceedings, doing whatever they could to avoid going to trial, and hoping for a stay. Their mantra was, "Delay, delay, delay."

"What do you think?" Paul asked me.

All the legal jargon they'd used in the process of explaining this to me was so far above my head, they might as well have been speaking Chinese. I felt powerless, which always makes me feel a little anxious, but I had to trust that they knew what they were doing. In the army, you learn to do your job as well as you can and have faith that those around you are doing the same. To me, this situation didn't seem all that much different.

"You know what? You guys are the professionals. I'll do whatever you think is best. I'm happy to defer to you."

FOR MY FINAL COURT APPEARANCE in the special Sessions Court the Ministry of Justice had set up inside the prison, I was placed inside a cage. That's right, a cage. It was made of steel, was located beside the judge's bench, and faced out into the room. It was also locked tight, but the guard who'd guided me into it still insisted on sitting inside it with me during the trial. I wasn't sure if this was to protect everyone in the room from me or me from them. Both, I imagined.

Whenever I'd appeared in court before, I'd gotten the sense that everyone in the room was just waiting for the judge to say I was guilty, so they could drag me outside and hang me from a tree, and this time was no different. The atmosphere in the claustrophobic little room was tense, almost hostile. But one important element of that court appearance did differ from all my previous ones: Asad Manzoor Butt, the prosecuting attorney who'd been riding me hard since day one, who'd claimed I'd shot Faizan Haider in the back despite not having any evidence to prove it, who'd once called me a vicious dog, who'd been so central to the drama during every one of my court appearances—suddenly this man wasn't there.

As odd as Butt's absence was, we weren't given long to dwell on it, as Raja Irshad, a former deputy attorney general who'd argued before the Supreme Court for six years earlier in his career and now worked for ISI and Pakistan's Military Intelligence, immediately stepped in to fill the void. Irshad looked like a Pakistani Abraham Lincoln, sporting Lincoln's full-beard, no-mustache look and wearing *shalwar kameez*. If his traditional, conservative dress didn't give away his political leanings, his 2008 admission that his son had been killed while fighting American forces alongside the Taliban in Afghanistan soon after 9/11 did; he was no friend of mine, or of any other American, for that matter.

Although Irshad was a lot shorter than Lincoln was reputed to be, his lack of height didn't diminish his authority in any way. In fact, you could tell how much influence and power he must have had just by the way he carried himself and the respect he was given by others. It was hard to take your eyes off him, as he, my attorneys, and the judge discussed my case at the front of the room. I couldn't follow what they were saying, and perhaps that was just as well because, while I'd been prepared for what resulted from their conversation, it still came as a bit of a shock to hear it spoken out loud.

I'd been officially charged with murder.

REPORTERS WEREN'T ALLOWED inside the courtroom, but word quickly traveled to where they were milling out in the hallway. They rushed to write their articles about how I was now one step closer to the gallows, but those who actually filed their pieces were much too hasty because the story was still unfolding. This became apparent to me when the judge cleared the courtroom of all extraneous personnel.

One of the few people allowed to stay behind was General Pasha, who'd been continually texting Ambassador Munter, updating him about the court proceedings. I imagine that at least one of his texts described the entrance of a man in a suit, whom I recognized but whose name I couldn't recall. As soon as this man entered the courtroom, the room went silent. No one spoke a word. If a cell phone rang, the person to whom it belonged got up and walked outside to answer it. The only thing you could hear was the ceiling fan. The response this man's presence got was strange but also oddly familiar.

Carmela and my team of attorneys were sitting directly in front of the cage, and I leaned forward, got Paul's attention, and pointed to the man in the suit. "Who is that guy?"

"Him? He's an ISI colonel. Why?"

I nodded. "Yeah, I thought so. He questioned me at the police station in Cantonment the day of the incident. I figured he was ISI. Why's he here?"

"He's a fixer."

"What's that mean?"

"Let me put it this way. It's either really good that he's here," Paul took a deep breath, "or really bad."

Maybe my experience had led me to embrace the power of positive thinking. Or maybe I was still feeling the effects of the double dose of coffee I'd enjoyed earlier. Whatever the reason, I couldn't help smiling and making light of the situation.

"Well," I said, grinning at Paul, "let's hope for option number one."

WHAT DID IT FEEL LIKE to be on trial for murder in Pakistan? It reminded me a little of the first time I jumped out of a plane. Both experiences were unquestionably terrifying, but dwelling on my fear only increased it. Letting go of it allowed a kind of stillness to take root. As the lawyers discussed my case in hushed tones and solely in Urdu, I was surprised by my reaction. Usually I would have interrupted them, asking them to speak louder and in English, but this time I let it go. My protestations hadn't gotten me very far in the past, and, besides, I had a team of lawyers now, and that was their job, right?

Still, I was happy when Paul broke free from the scrum of lawyers and ran over to give me an update. "Change of plans," he said, trying to catch his breath. "The judge has changed this to a Sharia court."

After getting over the initial shock, a barrage of images entered my head, none of them good. Flogging. Amputation. Death by stoning. Death by beheading. Crucifixion. An eye for an eye. There was no way I was getting an impartial trial in a Sharia court. This was beyond unfair. I was angry, but I was also terrified.

"What the hell, man? Are you serious? How can they do that? I don't understand."

But before the last few words were even out of my mouth, Paul had already turned around and run back to the scrum.

30.

KOT LAKHPAT JAIL, LAHORE, PAKISTAN
(March 16, 2011—Day 49)

THROUGHOUT MY ENTIRE ORDEAL, Carmela was the one person I could always count on. She'd been there for me from the very beginning and had fought for me every step of the way. She was a tireless advocate for my cause, and I could always trust her to make bad things better, if not disappear entirely. She'd worked overtime on my case, so it was no surprise that she was sitting in the first row of seats directly in front of my cage, as close to me as one could possibly get. I waved at her to get her attention.

"What's going on here, Carmela?"

"They've switched to Sharia law, Ray."

"I can't believe they can get away with this. I'm toast, right? They're going to drag me into this prison's courtyard and stone me to death, aren't they?"

"No, Ray. That's *qisas*. Sharia law also allows for *diyat*, which the families of the victims have agreed to accept."

I could hear words coming out of her mouth, but they made no sense to me. "*Qisas? Diyat?* Huh?"

"*Qisas* basically means 'an eye for an eye,' with the punishment effectively matching the offense. Those found guilty of murder are killed."

I gulped because I assumed this would be my fate. As an American accused of being a spy, how could I expect anything better? The signs held by the religious extremists while they protested in the streets made their desires clear. They wanted to see me dead. They wanted an eye for an eye. They wanted—no, they *demanded*—*qisas*.

Carmela must have seen the fear in my eyes because she hurriedly continued. "There's also *diyat*, also known as 'blood money.' In this case compensation gets paid to the victim or the victim's heirs, and the accused goes free. That's what's going to happen here. The victims' families are going to receive a sum of money, then you'll be getting released." She paused as if to emphasize what she was about to say next. "Ray, you're getting out of here!"

This was not what I expected to hear, and it took me a second to process the information. I was getting out! I was getting out? It didn't seem possible. Because of the many times I'd been given hope, only to have it yanked away at the last second, I remained wary. I wasn't going to start celebrating until my boots were firmly planted on American soil. Until then, I was going to remain cautious and be on the lookout for any shenanigans the Pakistanis might try to pull. Also, from what Carmela had just said, it sounded like my freedom was being bought, and I didn't like the sound of that at all.

"We shouldn't have to pay any money to get me out of here. I didn't do anything wrong."

"No, Ray, you don't understand. This is the *only* way we can get you out of here. It's not going to happen any other way. We've exhausted all our options and are down to this one. It's the best deal you're going to get. You have to take it. *We* have to take it."

If someone else had told me this, I might have argued with them. But I trusted Carmela. If she said I had to take the deal, then that's what I was going to do. "All right, fine. You're in charge. Go ahead and do whatever you feel needs to be done."

Any relief I might have felt—and there wasn't much because so much of this process was foreign to me—was interrupted when the judge asked the prison superintendent to "summon the legal heirs of the deceased," who were lingering outside. The few witnesses allowed to remain inside the courtroom all turned their heads and murmured as a door in the back of the courtroom opened and eighteen relatives of the two men I'd shot stepped inside and, one by one, started walking toward the front of the room. Because a row of police officers had been placed in front of the cage I was in, shielding me from view, I couldn't really see them and they couldn't really see me.

I glanced at Carmela, hoping to get a better idea of what was going to happen next, and I could tell by the way she was chewing on her lip that she was nervous. "What's wrong, Carmela?"

"Every single one them needs to agree to the deal for it to happen. If even one of them decides not to go through with it, the whole arrangement falls through." She glanced at the procession of family members. "And the women do not look happy at all."

AS CHARITABLE AS *diyat* might seem when compared to *qisas*, the practice has proved to be extremely controversial in Pakistan, as it's frequently been used to provide legal protection to those who've carried out so-called honor killings. Some Islamic fundamentalists believe that murdering a family member who has brought shame to your household—typically a woman accused of committing adultery—can restore honor to your family. More than 1,000 Pakistani women are killed in this manner each year.

Relying on such a law to secure my freedom wouldn't have been my first choice. As someone who values the separation of church and state, I found Sharia law repugnant. But, as Carmela had made perfectly clear, I really didn't have a say in the matter.

From what I later found out, the plan had been hatched several weeks before. Some reports trace its origin to John Kerry's visit with Husain Haqqani, Pakistan's ambassador to the United States, four weeks earlier. Another account said the plan had been devised during a meeting between General Pasha and Ambassador Munter. The Pakistani military was also rumored to have had a hand in it. So, too, President Zardari and Nawaz Sharif. Peter Strasser brought up the idea as soon as he was enlisted to assemble my legal counsel. Bukhari did as well. In the end, no one individual should receive the credit for devising the plan. It was clearly a group effort. Everyone involved knew that it offered both sides the best way to extricate themselves from the diplomatic crisis without losing face. Everyone, it seemed, but me. I was kept in the dark until the very last moment.

Once the plan was hatched, it was up to ISI to carry it out, but a Pakistani officer was more than happy to let me twist in the wind all the way up until the very end. At the same time, Pasha was clearly committed to making sure that the deal was successful. He'd been scheduled to retire on March 18, but, given all that he had on his plate, he agreed to remain in his position for another year. He was also responsible for replacing the prosecutor, Asad Manzoor Butt—who, according to one report, had worked the case pro bono at the behest of the conservative Islamist political party *Jamaat-e-Islami*—with Raja Irshad, who was more beholden to ISI than any religious group.

Because the plan hinged on the acquiescence of the eighteen family members, ISI agents applied as much pressure as was needed to get them to accept the *diyat*. With the support of their lawyer, Butt, several of them resisted. One of those who didn't accept the plan right away was Muhammad Faheem's brother, Waseem Shamzad. Buoyed by the long line of Islamist politicians who'd come to his ramshackle house and urged him to seek justice over blood money, he didn't come onboard for weeks.

Another dissenter was Mashhood-ur-Rehman, whose brother had been killed by the SUV coming to rescue me and who'd recently obtained his law degree in the United Kingdom. "I can't straight away accept money," he said in the days leading up to my trial. "It's a question of family honor. There has to be something toward justice first."

To separate the family members from the radical Islamists whispering in their ears and the lawyer who endorsed a hardline Islamist agenda, ISI operatives intervened on March 14, detaining and sequestering all eighteen of them. For the two days preceding the March 16 trial that would decide my fate, Butt was unable to reach any of them by phone, and their neighbors confirmed that they had disappeared.

"There is a padlock on their door," said Faizan Haider's cousin Aijaz Ahmad. "Their phones are all switched off. If they have done this, then they have acted dishonorably."

The night before the March 16 trial, ISI agents took the family members to Kot Lakhpat Jail and encouraged them to accept the deal that was on the table. If they agreed to forgive me, they would be given a large sum of money in return. If they didn't agree, well, the consequences of that decision were made clear the following morning when they were reportedly held at gunpoint just outside the prison's courtroom for several hours and warned not to say a word about it to the media.

When Butt arrived at the prison that morning, he received similar treatment. "I was not allowed to participate in the proceedings of the case

... and could not see or approach my clients," he told the BBC afterward. "I and my associate were kept under forced detention for four hours."

Butt was never able to see or talk to any of his (now former) clients. The shock of being denied access to the man who'd guided them through their country's convoluted legal system for more than a month, and forced to agree to a deal that many of them didn't want, was evident on their faces as they shuffled to the front of the courtroom on March 16. And, as Carmela had observed, the women were indeed the ones taking it the hardest. Some of them had tears in their eyes. Others were sobbing outright.

Their new lawyer, Irshad, presented the judge with a signed document showing that all eighteen of Muhammad Faheem and Faizan Haider's legal heirs had agreed, at least on paper, to forgive me and accept the *diyat*. For all its old-world charm, the process was actually more bureaucratic than anything. The judge asked the relatives to present documents proving their identity, then gave each of them a receipt showing the amount of money that was to be doled out: $130,000 each for a total of $2,340,000, the largest amount of blood money ever awarded in Pakistan.

After each relative had signed the necessary paperwork, the judge asked if any of them had been coerced into doing it. All eighteen relatives said no. The judge also reminded both the defense and the prosecution that they were entitled to object. Neither side did.

Because that day's court proceedings were conducted entirely in Urdu for the benefit of the family members, most, if not all, of what took place was beyond my comprehension. Luckily, Carmela was there to guide me.

"All of them accepted the *diyat*, Ray. You're getting out of here."

"Really? When?"

"As soon as we're done here, you're going to get into a vehicle that's waiting for you outside. Dale's going to go with you to the airport and oversee a medical test you need to take, then you're going to get on a plane and fly home."

I was a little dazed by the sudden acceleration of time. My mind had grown accustomed to everything being a long, drawn-out process. I was used to things moving slowly. I'd assumed that after we left the courtroom we were going to head straight into another meeting. So to have it all come to an end so suddenly was a real shock to my system, like rolling in snow after lounging in a hot tub for several hours.

"Wait a minute. I'm leaving *today*?"

"Yes, Ray. You're free. You're going home."

That's when it really sunk in. I'd gotten so used to suppressing my emotions that when I finally allowed them to surface they hit me with the force of a tsunami. For forty-nine days, I'd lived moment to moment, never allowing myself to get too high or too low. I'd mentally prepared myself to be incarcerated for a very long time, and up to this point, I'd done a good job of managing my expectations and doing whatever needed to be done to get through the day.

But the moment I realized that I was actually being released, that it wasn't some cruel joke, I let my guard down and allowed all the emotions I'd kept at bay—joy, shock, sadness, fear—to return. Because of my occupation and my physical appearance, I was viewed as a tough guy, but now during one of the most intense and vulnerable minutes of my life, all that toughness disappeared, and I was just a husband and a father who wanted nothing more than to go home.

And, yes, I cried. I cried like a baby.

31.

HIGHLANDS RANCH, COLORADO
(March 16, 2011—Day 49)

T HERE WAS A KNOCK ON MY FRONT DOOR *at 6:30 in the morning. When I opened it, I saw one of the guys Ray worked with standing there. He didn't say a word. He didn't have to. It had to be bad news. This was the awful knock I'd always dreaded. Why else would someone come to your house at 6:30 in the morning?*

"Is Ray dead?" The way I said it, just blurting it out with no emotion attached, must have shocked the guy. I wasn't crying. I wasn't hysterical. In fact, I probably came off sounding a little cold and businesslike. I couldn't help it. After all I'd been through, waiting forty-nine days to find out whether my husband was ever coming home, this was just my way of coping with the situation. "Give it to me straight. Don't sugarcoat it. Just tell me what happened, so I can do what I need to do. Is he dead?"

"No, he's out! They just released him!"

AS SOON AS IT REGISTERED THAT RAY WAS FREE and on his way home, I felt so relieved. It was like a giant weight had been lifted off my shoulders. But as exciting as the news was, Ray was still more than 7,000 miles away, and until he walked through the front door I still had a household to run. They say kids need predictable routines, and I didn't see any good reason to alter my son's until Ray was actually home, so I dropped him off at his preschool just like I always did.

When I got back to the house, things were anything but routine. There were trucks and cameras and microphones all over the place, three or four times as many as there'd ever been before, and as soon as I pulled into the driveway, the reporters and cameramen descended upon me.

I don't like being the center of attention. It makes me very uncomfortable because whenever I'm speaking to a large group of people I always feel like I come across the wrong way or I'm misunderstood. But given the news I'd heard earlier, I knew I had to say something to the press. I understood how bad it would look if I were captured on film saying, "No comment, no comment, no comment," as I ran into my house the day my husband was released from prison. Hoping to get it over with as quickly as possible, I asked all the reporters to gather in a semicircle in my front yard, so I could address them all at once.

They immediately started bombarding me with questions, and from the tone of their questions I got the sense that they wanted me to say and do certain things. They wanted me to tell them how happy I was. They wanted me to say that I was overjoyed because my husband was free and safe and coming home. But I was really nervous, and when I get nervous sometimes I ramble. I hope I succeeded in getting across what had been missing from all of their stories—that Ray was cool-headed and even-tempered, a sweet man who wouldn't hurt a fly unless he absolutely had to—and from the few sound bites I've heard I believe I did.

"I knew that he did what he had to do because he had to do it," I told a local TV station. "It was kill or be killed."

When a reporter from CNN tried to poke a hole in my assessment of Ray, I was happy to be given the opportunity to defend him. "I knew it was self-defense. My husband's not a killer. He's not a Rambo like the L.A. Times said. He's not an agent. He's not Jason Bourne. He's not any of these kind of crazy things that have been portrayed of him."

Because these responses lined up perfectly with what they were seeking—a dutiful wife standing by her brave, patriotic husband—they made it on TV. But there were plenty of awkward and uncomfortable moments that didn't. Some of the reporters kept asking questions that had nothing to do with the incident. They wanted to know about Ray's contract with Blackwater years before and tried to make a connection between that and the incident in Lahore when there simply wasn't one.

Another reporter raised the issue of the $2,340,000 in blood money that had been awarded to the families of the two men Ray had shot, asking me who'd actually paid it and how it had been delivered, as if I'd know. I didn't even know the exact amount that had been paid until one of the reporters informed me. Upon hearing the sum, I feigned indignation, then started laughing. "That's it?" I said. "That's all he's worth?"

That's *why I don't like talking to large groups of people. Sometimes I get so nervous I say some of the dumbest things.*

Making the situation even worse, I think they wanted—no, they expected—*me to cry, but I was long past that. I was obviously happy that Ray was coming home. I was especially happy for my son. But the romantic love Ray and I once shared just wasn't there anymore. It wasn't his fault. I blame his job, and I blame the war. Ray can be the nicest person in the world, but after being exposed to so much ugliness and evil and insanity while working overseas, I think it changed him. I mean, how could it not? He was still a nice guy, but he wasn't the same person I married. I feel like the War on Terror stole him from me and my son.*

Adding to my anxiety, I didn't feel like I had any right to complain about Ray's extended absences from home because of the sacrifice he was making for our family. He put his life on the line every day he was on the job, and as much as he was doing it for our country, he was also doing it for me and our son. To pay our bills, to put food on our table. So even just feeling that way made me feel guilty. But eventually I got over that and realized that it was okay for me to be mad, that I had a right to be mad. Because the war affected me, too, just as it affected everyone who was close to Ray. It just affected us in a totally different way than it affected him. For much of the year he had to live in an environment where he could be killed at any second, and the rest of the time we had to live with a person who'd lived in such a place.

Whenever he came home after being overseas, I would beg him to choose—me or his job—and he always chose his job. He may have done it for honorable reasons—serving his country and providing for his family being the main ones—but it still hurt. As much pain as his decision brought me, I also respected him for it because very few people have the ability to make that choice. I admired the fact that he was able to stay true to himself. Sure, I wish he'd chosen to stay with me and our son, but, ultimately, that wasn't what he wanted. I know he loved us, but he loved his job even more. It really was his passion, and you can't do that sort of work and be Father of the Year at the same time. You can't be over there working to protect our country and still be home for dinner every night at six and coach youth soccer on the weekends. You just can't. You've got to choose. And he chose that life.

I tend to wear my emotions on my sleeve. I'm a terrible liar. But I knew I couldn't tell the reporters who were bunched together in my front yard how I really felt. Not then. Not on national TV. Not on the day I found out my husband was coming home. So I did my best to hide my true feelings, and having to do that made me even more nervous. That morning was extremely awkward and uncomfortable for me. The reporters wanted me to cry, but all I could do was laugh.

32.

KOT LAKHPAT JAIL, LAHORE, PAKISTAN
(March 16, 2011—Day 49)

D URING A VISIT TO CAIRO later that same day, National Public Radio's
Steve Inskeep asked Secretary of State Hillary Clinton if paying blood
money to get me released was a good idea.

"Well, first of all, the United States did not pay any compensation,"
she responded. "The families of the victims of the incident on January
27 decided to pardon Mr. Davis. And we are very grateful for their decision. And we are very grateful to the people and government of Pakistan,
who have a very strong relationship with us that we are committed to
strengthening."

Inskeep pressed her about the origins of the blood money.

"The United States did not pay any compensation," Clinton reiterated.

Technically, what she said was true. According to the *New York Times*,
ISI paid the money, and the US government later reimbursed the Pakistani government.

ISI also orchestrated my exit. Several agents led me out of the courtroom through a back entrance. We were walking in the direction of my
cell when it occurred to me that I had to pee really badly. I'd been forced
to sit in that cage for the past five or six hours without a single break.

"Can I use the bathroom in my cell before we go to the next meeting?" I asked.

"I'm sorry, sir. We don't have time."

"You don't understand. I've been stuck inside that courtroom all day
long. I really need to go."

He flashed his partner a concerned look and sighed. "Okay, but you must be quick."

They led me to my cell but didn't allow me very much time. "Come on, let's go, hurry up," they kept saying over and over again until I was finished.

I didn't understand what the big hurry was. I assumed I would be meeting with the consulate personnel one more time before I took off some time later in the day. I was acting like I had all the time in the world, but the agents had a very different mindset. As soon as I was done using the bathroom, they hustled me down a hallway and to a door that led outside. I didn't even have a chance to grab any of my things out of my cell.

Standing beside the closed door, I could hear the distinctive sound of an SUV's diesel engine, and I knew without anyone having to tell me that it was waiting for me. That's when it dawned on me: I wasn't leaving later today; I was leaving *right now*.

Suddenly, I was the one who was in a hurry. "Let's go, let's go," I said to the men who'd been leading me.

"Please wait here, sir."

One of the men opened the door, stepped out into a courtyard, and scanned the horizon as if looking for a possible ambush. Once he'd cleared the area, I was waved through the door and directed to the SUV idling in the courtyard. As I fast-walked across the courtyard, I encouraged the men on either side of me to pick up the pace.

When I finally reached the SUV, I was a little hesitant at first because I didn't see Dale Rush, the doctor from the embassy who I'd bonded with during my time in jail and who Carmela said would be there. I only saw two men who looked Pakistani, and I didn't recognize either one of them. The men standing on either side of me opened one of the SUV's back doors and tried to push me inside the vehicle, but I refused to be moved. If Dale wasn't here, then something must be wrong. My instinct was to wait for him to arrive before getting in, so I just stood there, holding my ground, until the driver turned around and said, "I'm from the US Embassy. It's an honor to drive you." That was enough to convince me to get in.

The man in the passenger seat was busy talking on his phone. As soon as he was done, I said to him, "And who are you?"

He turned around and stared at me. "I am the Colonel."

I couldn't believe I was going down this road again, but I decided to play along. "Colonel *who?*"

"I am the Colonel."

These ISI officers were so transparent it almost made me laugh.

AS WE STARTED DRIVING, the high walls of the prison made it feel like we were traveling through a maze. I was beginning to think we might never get out of there, especially after getting stopped by an enormous gate. When it opened, I saw Dale standing on the other side. I started to get out of the SUV, thinking in my confusion that this was where the medical test was going to be, but Dale ran up to the door and pushed me back inside.

"Get in, get in," he yelled.

I didn't understand what the big fuss was about. "Whoa, what's going on, Dale?"

He started pushing me down onto the floorboard. "Get down on the floor. Now."

"What the heck are you doing, Dale?"

"You need to get down and stay down. We don't want anyone from the media to see you leave."

Trusting that he knew what he was doing, I lowered myself to the floor and pressed myself against it. No easy task, given my size.

As we drove through the gate, several other vehicles joined us, forming a convoy. There was one vehicle directly in front of us and one directly behind us. As far as I could tell, no one else was following us, and yet Dale still seemed really nervous. I could hear it in his voice.

"It's okay," he said to me. "Just stay down. We're going to be all right. We're going to be fine."

"Dale, calm down, man. What are you so worried about?"

He leaned down and whispered, "Sorry, I've just never done anything like this before."

Dale's nervousness had a pronounced effect on me, but not in the way you might think. It actually calmed me down. Knowing that I wasn't truly free until I'd gotten out of Pakistan, I was also very anxious, but I knew that one of us needed to be level-headed. I imagined that important decisions would still need to be made, and if we weren't thinking clearly whatever plan had been created to smuggle me out of the country would have a greater chance of falling apart.

"Look, everything's going to be just fine. I promise you. You don't have to worry about a thing."

He nodded. "Wait, aren't I supposed to be the one reassuring you?"

I shrugged.

After a few minutes, he said, "Okay, you can sit up now."

I did, and with a glance out the window I could tell exactly where we were.

Dale pulled out a phone. "I need to call the boss."

I nodded and continued to study the road ahead.

"We've left the prison," he said into the phone. "We're on our way to the airport."

After nodding his head a few times, Dale pressed the phone to his chest, muffling its receiver, and asked aloud, "How far from the airport are we?"

There was no response from the front of the vehicle.

I looked out the window. "We're about fifteen minutes away, Dale."

He gave me a weird look before relaying the information to the boss.

Ten minutes later, Dale started to look really nervous again. "How far away are we now?"

"About five minutes," I told him.

Five minutes later, we pulled into the airport, and Dale looked at me as if seeing me for the first time. "You really do know your way around here," he whispered.

I shrugged. "Just part of the job, man."

AS SOON AS WE CAME TO A STOP, Dale grabbed me. "All right, here's what's going to happen. We're going to go inside, and you're going to get checked out by a Pakistani doctor. Once you're done with that, you need to get dressed as fast as you can because we'll be getting onto an airplane and taking off as soon as possible after that. Got it?"

I nodded to show him that I understood, and Dale led me inside a building and into a room where a doctor was waiting for me. One of the men from the two vehicles that escorted us to the airport followed us into the room and captured everything I did on video—evidence, I supposed, that I was unharmed. Even after the doctor asked me to remove my clothes, the man continued to film me.

Oh, great, I thought. *I bet this is going to find its way onto the Internet somehow.*

After thoroughly examining me, the doctor determined I was physically fit and didn't have any injuries. "There's just one thing I need before I can let you go. Can you show me an identifiable mark?"

"What do you mean?"

"Something on your body that someone close to you could identify. Like a tattoo. Do you have any tattoos?"

Still completely naked, I lifted my arms and turned around so he could see every inch of me. "Do you see any tattoos?"

"How about a scar then?"

All I could do was stare at him. I did have some scars on my body, but I thought pointing them out to him contradicted the goal of the task. If he couldn't find them himself, then they really weren't much use as identifiable marks, now were they?

"I can't let you leave here until you show me some sort of identifiable mark."

I could tell Dale was getting agitated, even more so than before, and his anxiety was starting to rub off on me. I frantically searched my body for something someone else might recognize and settled on a pea-sized freckle on my chest.

"Oh, look," I said, hopefully. "A mole."

"That's it," Dale said to the doctor. "He's got a mole on his chest." He scooped up my clothes and thrust them at me. "Now get dressed so we can get out of here."

I was putting my clothes back on as fast as I could, but it obviously wasn't fast enough for Dale. I hadn't even pulled my pants all the way up or buttoned my shirt when he grabbed my arm and started dragging me toward the door.

"C'mon, Dale. Let me finish getting dressed. It's embarrassing enough being filmed naked. I'd at least like to be wearing *some* clothes when I walk out of here."

"We don't have time. You can get dressed on the plane. We need to go. *Now.*"

33.

KABUL AIRSPACE

(March 16, 2011—Day 49)

A DUAL-ENGINE CESSNA WAS WAITING for us on the runway. With its engines running, the prop plane was all set to take off. It just needed its final two passengers, me and Dale, to board. As I ran toward the plane, I was still buttoning my shirt and hoping I wouldn't trip over my untied shoelaces, which were flopping against the tarmac.

An older man in a suit was waiting at the bottom of the stairs that led up into the plane. When I reached him, he stuck out his hand. I shook it and, without thinking about it, pulled him into my chest for a second the same way I would have with one of my close friends. A woman stepped out of the man's shadow and formally introduced him to me.

"Ray, this is Cameron Munter," the diplomatic agent said before clarifying his identity for me. "The US ambassador to Pakistan."

Typical me: I'd just given the highest-ranking US diplomat in Pakistan a bro hug. I couldn't stop apologizing.

The ambassador told me not to worry about it. He even insisted on carrying one of my bags—the heavy one!—up the stairs for me. Use of this plane was one of the perks of being ambassador, he told me, although I didn't understand why he was leaving the country, too. After giving it some thought, I decided that, in an odd twist, he was providing security for me. With the ambassador onboard the plane, the Pakistanis wouldn't dare mess around with it by denying it clearance to take off due to some bureaucratic error or—who knows?—tipping off some militant group that might try to shoot it out of the sky. The ambassador was there to ensure that I got out of the country smoothly.

Dale's role was just as simple and every bit as necessary. The DOD's Joint Personnel Recovery Agency, whose job it was to help me reintegrate into normal life after being held captive for so long, had suggested that he accompany me on the plane ride from Lahore so that he could be there to reassure me, provide continuity, and be a familiar face. Because he'd been there since Day One—well, actually Day Two—he was somebody I knew and trusted. His presence was an important part of the repatriation process. And the fact that he was a doctor certainly didn't hurt.

As soon as we were all on board and seated, one of the three members of the flight crew pulled the door closed and locked it, and the plane started taxiing down the runway. As we passed the SUV that had delivered me to the airport and was now parked on the edge of the tarmac, the ISI colonel said goodbye with a weary salute.

Despite the last-minute reprieve I enjoyed in the courtroom, I didn't feel entirely free yet because I was still in Pakistan, but I knew that was about to change. In my head I eagerly counted down the seconds until my departure. You know that rush of excitement you get just as you're about to take off in a plane on your way to a much-needed vacation in some exotic location? Multiply that by a thousand, and you'll get a sense of how I was feeling at that moment. I was going home!

If the ambassador shared my enthusiasm, he didn't show it. He was all business. It was early afternoon when we took off from the airport in Lahore, and nine hours behind in Washington, DC, people were just starting to wake up. The ambassador wanted the American press to have the correct story when they shuffled into the office—that I was free and safe and on my way home—and not the one that had already been filed by so many overeager Pakistani journalists just a few hours before—that I'd been charged with double homicide and would be tried for murder. As much as the ambassador wanted the real story to get out, he also knew he didn't want to relay that news until I was actually out of Pakistani airspace. It would have looked really bad if the story got picked up by the media and our plane was forced to turn around and return to Lahore for some reason.

"How long until we reach Kabul airspace?" he asked one of the members of the flight crew once we were in the air.

"One hour and forty-five minutes, sir."

An hour later, he asked the same question.

"An hour and ten minutes, sir."

"What? How can that be?"

"We're flying into a very strong headwind, sir. It's really slowing us down."

"Oh, great," I said. "There's a vortex over Pakistan that won't let me leave. It's trying to suck me back in."

I was trying to be funny, but Dale was the only one who laughed. He'd come to know and appreciate my occasionally morbid sense of humor, which was reason enough to have him onboard. I was making small talk with him and the ambassador's diplomatic agent, and we must have gotten really into it because the next thing I knew the flight crew was handing me a plaque with a knife on it, a bottle, and a folded-up piece of paper.

"We'd like to give you a few gifts, Ray. You did a hell of a job sticking in there like that."

I opened the piece of paper and found a coin taped to the inside. Inscribed on it were the words, "Welcome to Kabul airspace."

Now I could celebrate. I'd made it. I was free.

THE AMBASSADOR TOOK THE OPPORTUNITY to make a few calls with his satellite phone. He wanted to share the news that I'd been released with some of the people who'd been so heavily invested in getting me out, a list that included Senator John Kerry, Congressman Frank Wolf, and US Special Representative for Afghanistan and Pakistan Marc Grossman, the man who'd succeeded the highly respected American diplomat Richard Holbrooke. During a lull between calls, the ambassador handed me his phone.

"It's the secretary of state. If you wouldn't mind, could you put in a few good words for me and my people?"

I cleared my throat and racked my brain for the proper way to address her. "Uh, hello, Madam Secretary."

The dreamlike quality of my day continued as the distinctive sound of Hillary Clinton's overly scrutinized voice responded from the other end of the line. "It's so good to hear your voice and know that you're safe. We're so proud of you."

"I appreciate it, ma'am, and I just want to let you know that I'm grateful for everything your people did for me. They were incredible. You couldn't have picked a better team to help me get through that situation. I'm truly grateful they were there to help me."

Everything else that was said during that brief conversation remains a blur. Having provided security for some of the highest-ranking officials in the United States, I usually don't get awed in their presence, but I have to admit that speaking to the secretary of state on the phone had my head spinning.

After the buzz from that conversation had worn off and all the hubbub surrounding our hurried exit from Pakistan had died down, Dale tapped me on the shoulder. "Hey, I've got a question for you. Why did you wear that blue fleece all the time?"

"Huh?"

"You wore a blue fleece to almost all of our meetings."

"Oh, yeah, I guess I did."

"It really concerned us because, you know, 'blue' is a code word for distress."

The laugh that escaped me surprised me with its intensity. I hadn't laughed so hard in forty-nine days, and it was full of relief and joy. "That didn't even enter my mind. I wore it because I was cold. It was about twenty degrees inside that prison, and it was the only warm thing I had!"

Epilogue

M Y RELEASE DIDN'T PLEASE EVERYONE. On April 11, General Pasha flew to Washington to relay Islamabad's concerns to Leon Panetta and Admiral Mike Mullen, but any progress made during that meeting disappeared three weeks later when American forces carried out a raid on the compound in Abbottabad that left Osama bin Laden dead. The assessment that Admiral William McRaven had made four months earlier had been dead on: Breaching the walls of the compound and taking out bin Laden wouldn't be all that difficult, but appeasing the Pakistani government afterward would be.

Pakistani officials responded much as they were expected to, arguing that this top-secret, unilateral mission violated their nation's sovereignty. But after all the smoke had cleared, the onus was on them to explain how the world's most-wanted terrorist had been living within their borders for six years without anyone knowing about it—and just a mile from Pakistan's premier military academy, no less! Instead of assuming any responsibility for bin Laden's presence in their country, they went on the offensive, with Foreign Secretary Salman Bashir declaring that a similar raid in the future could lead to "terrible consequences." Later that same month, Robert Blackwill, the US Ambassador to India for two years immediately following 9/11, came right out and said what so many American officials were thinking, that "the Pakistani military is not an ally, not a partner, not a friend of the US." Two months later, the United States made it official by suspending $800 million in military aid.

In the months following my release from Kot Lakhpat Jail, US–Pakistani relations hit one of the lowest points in their long, volatile history, bringing to mind the tension that followed the 1979 burning and ransacking of the US Embassy in Islamabad. Even though I'd acted in self-defense, I still couldn't help thinking that I'd contributed more than my fair share to the tension between the two countries. I don't regret shooting those two men in Lahore. I believe it was an appropriate response to a life-threatening situation. But I do regret the turmoil it created.

"If Pakistan had convicted an American who held diplomatic status, it would have been akin to the violation of diplomatic rules that took place in Tehran in 1979," Munter later said, referring to the Iranian Hostage Crisis, which saw a group of Iranian students storm the US Embassy in Tehran and hold more than sixty Americans hostage for 444 days. "Had we not been able to get Raymond Davis out, and especially if they had convicted Raymond Davis, it could have conceivably led to a breach in relations."

Fortunately, the persistent tension between the United States and Pakistan never reached that point. The situation was handled in such a way that most of the higher-level officials who were involved managed to come out the other side relatively unscathed. President Zardari actually completed his five-year term in office, becoming the first democratically elected Pakistani president ever to do so, while President Obama succeeded in getting reelected in November 2012. After a career filled with accolades, General Pasha retired in 2012, and the following year, General Kayani and Leon Panetta, after a short stint as secretary of defense, did likewise.

While the taint from the incident rolled off the backs of these politicians and military leaders like water off a duck, it would bring far more suffering to those who were closer to it. A little more than a year after I was released, the blood money given to the victims' families proved to be bloody indeed. Going from hopelessly poor to fabulously wealthy overnight allowed Faizan Haider's wife Zohra and her family to move from Lahore's low-rent Ferozewala neighborhood to the more upscale Johar Town, but it also had the same sort of negative effect on them that winning the lottery has had on so many others. Illiterate and unaccustomed to wealth, they were outcasts on a street filled with affluent and well-educated families. Zohra's father, Shahzad Butt, a former mechanic, stuck out the most, often climbing onto the roof of their new home and firing guns into the air. As dramatic as such displays were, they paled in comparison to the one that occurred on April 30, 2012, when Butt shot and killed his daughter Zohra and his wife Nabeela Bibi in a dispute over money after Zohra announced her plans to remarry.

"These people were low-status, both financially and in terms of caste," their former lawyer Asad Manzoor Butt commented. "They had no idea how to cope with that sort of money."

The incident in Lahore had a similarly ruinous impact on my life. The first thing I had to do upon returning to the United States was talk with investigators from the DOJ about the shooting. In my heart and in my mind I'd done nothing wrong, but John Kerry had promised the Pakistanis that the incident would be thoroughly investigated, so I had no choice. Two guys with briefcases sat me down in a room and asked me to tell them my story from A to Z, from the minute I woke up on January 27 to the moment I was arrested by the police.

It was a frustrating process because the investigators kept trying to poke holes in my story. They would make small but meaningful changes to my statement, and I would have to retell that part of the story over and over again to make sure they had it right. This kept happening, and it was extremely annoying. I knew they were just doing their jobs, but the way they went about it made me feel like I was back in Pakistan getting interrogated by the police. It was as if they were trying to trip me up or catch me in a lie, and after several hours of this, I'd finally had enough. I told them they could charge me with a crime or let me go, but, either way, I was done speaking with them.

They stared at me for a second, put their pens down, closed their books, said, "Thank you very much, Mr. Davis," and walked out of the room.

Even though I never heard from them again and was found innocent of any wrongdoing, the incident in Lahore still succeeded in derailing my career. Unable to obtain the proper security clearance, I could no longer do any security contract work overseas. I often lament the passing of that phase of my life. To be prohibited from doing the job you've trained so long and hard to do takes a toll on you mentally and emotionally. A bullet hadn't stopped me. An IED wasn't to blame. But at the end of the day, the result was the same: I was never going to be an Old Warrior.

I remember turning to Rebecca one day and throwing my hands in the air in frustration. "What am I supposed to do now?" I said. "I only know how to shoot guns and blow things up."

But at the same time, I realize how lucky I am to simply be alive and whole. Many of my former colleagues weren't so fortunate. One of the guys I trained with before my first contracting job died within six months of his arrival in Iraq. Suicide bombers used backpacks to smuggle bombs inside the Green Zone, and the blast killed my friend and three other guys. One of them was so badly disfigured that rescuers couldn't positively identify his body until they found the serial number of his weapon imprinted on a wall.

That attack took place in 2004, one of the most dangerous years of the entire Iraq War. I was originally slated to go there that year, but at the last second I got rerouted to Afghanistan to be on Karzai's detail. I'd gotten lucky, I suppose, just as I had been for much of my career. I found myself in a number of tight spots during my time in the military and later in the private security-contracting business, none more so than the forty-nine days I spent incarcerated in Pakistan, but, all in all, I'd have to say that I've been blessed with a fairly full Luck Jar.

Having said that, the incident in Lahore did more than just strip me of my job. It very nearly succeeded in stealing my identity. I became so closely linked to the word "incident" that you might think it was actually part of my name. Go ahead and look me up on Wikipedia. You won't find me. But you will find the "Raymond Allen Davis incident." The conflation of my identity with the event that occurred on January 27, 2011, made me think during some of my worst moments that I was no longer an actual person but simply a historical footnote.

And what's written in that footnote often reflects poorly on my character. My name has been dragged through the mud so many times you need a hose to read it. I came to expect such treatment from the Pakistani newspapers, but I was shocked and dismayed to discover that the American media often lifted erroneous details from those accounts and presented them as facts. I suspect many Americans judged me based on those false reports, asking themselves why the US government would pay so much money to have me released when I'd been doing all these horrible things overseas.

Some people went so far as to compare me to Bowe Bergdahl, an association that still bothers me. Bergdahl walked off his post and surrendered to the Taliban, forcing our government to trade five Taliban prisoners to get him back, whereas I was captured while doing my job and, when given the opportunity to be traded for a terrorist, I refused. To anyone who's still unclear about what I was doing in Pakistan on January

27, 2011, I would simply say that I was there for the same reason I joined the army when I was eighteen years old: to support and defend the Constitution of the United States against all enemies, foreign and domestic. I wasn't some mercenary whose only desire was to make money. I was in Pakistan to protect the interests of the United States during the War on Terror and help preserve the American Dream.

Other people wanted to call me a hero, but I've never thought of myself that way. If I did anything noteworthy during my time in Kot Lakhpat Jail, it was simply surviving without letting the situation get to me too much. I've never wanted to exaggerate the importance of my role because, frankly, there's nothing beautiful about war. While being interviewed, some military guys like to brag about having put a red dot between someone's eyes and watching him go down. I'm not one of those guys. War has claimed the lives of too many people I've known and loved to make me ever want to glorify it. War kept me away from my family for far too long. And war eventually led to the dissolution of my marriage. Two years after the incident in Lahore, Rebecca and I agreed to an amicable, and yet still shocking and sad divorce. While all the time I'd spent working overseas had helped us pay our bills, it had also destroyed our relationship.

I can't say it enough: There's nothing beautiful about war.

What's beautiful is coming home and watching my kid run through the sprinklers, playing tag with him, seeing him laugh uncontrollably. That's beautiful. Nothing I did while working overseas was beautiful. I was just doing my job.

Acknowledgments

A s much as I'd like this book to serve as a snapshot of my experience in Lahore, Pakistan, during the first three months of 2011, I'm also hoping it will be received as a very long and heartfelt thank-you card by the State Department employees who devoted thousands of hours to defending my rights and orchestrating my release from prison. All the tireless work they did behind the scenes, the countless hours spent pulling paperwork, arranging meetings, and arguing on my behalf, did not go unnoticed.

One of my greatest fears in writing this book is that I may have failed to adequately portray the courage and commitment of the consulate staff who visited me nearly every single day I was in prison. In many ways, Carmela Conroy is the true hero of this story. I remain in awe of the toughness, intelligence, and dedication she displayed while working so doggedly to resolve my situation. A true diplomat, she never allowed the immensity of the task she faced to overwhelm her, despite spending nearly as many hours in Kot Lakhpat Jail as I did.

Displaying a similar commitment as well as a great sense of humor, Dale Rush provided much-needed entertainment and reassurance throughout my time in jail in addition to his medical knowledge. You're a true warrior, brother.

I'd also like to thank Cameron Munter and Peter Strasser, not just for the work they did to get me released but also for their willingness years later to answer the many questions I had about what took place behind the scenes while I was imprisoned. If they hadn't contributed their thoughts and opinions in their particular areas of expertise (diplomacy and law, respectively), this book would have suffered greatly, and for that I'm eternally grateful.

Shepherding this project from the idea stage all the way through to publication, Michael Wright displayed the full range of what a great literary agent can do. Without him and his partner, Leslie Garson, this book never would have found its way to print. Thank you for your support and the many hours you devoted to this project.

One of Michael's most astute choices was teaming me up with a co-author as skilled and dedicated as Storms Reback. He helped shape the disorganized memories I had of my time in Pakistan into the polished narrative you now hold in your hands. By Storms' own estimation, an equal amount of praise should go to his wife, Nissa Brown, who supported him with unwavering devotion, even as he continually disappeared into his office for days on end.

As a first-time author, I was initially intimidated by the publishing process, but everyone I worked with at BenBella Books set me at ease and impressed me with their talent and professionalism. The publisher, Glenn Yeffeth; the deputy publisher, Adrienne Lang; the editor in chief, Leah Wilson; the editor, Vy Tran; and the art director, Sarah Avinger, were particularly helpful, and I remain indebted to them for making this book the best it could possibly be.

It saddens me to think that my mother and father will never get to read this book, but I take solace in the fact that my brother and sister will. Their love and support mean everything to me.

Most marriages that end in divorce also end in acrimony; luckily, mine did not. Rebecca Davis remains a good friend, and I can't thank her enough for her many contributions to this book. I'm especially grateful to her for sharing her insight into what life was like at home while I was languishing in jail, and if it hasn't been clear how much I appreciate all the time and effort she's devoted to raising our son, I hope it is now.

About the Authors

Raymond Davis served in the US Army for nearly a decade, more than half of it as a member of Special Forces. After an injury forced him out of the army, he worked as a private security contractor in Iraq, Afghanistan, and Pakistan. This is his first book.

Storms Reback is the author of three books, including *Ship It Holla Ballas!: How a Bunch of 19-Year-Old College Dropouts Used the Internet to Become Poker's Loudest, Craziest, and Richest Crew*. He lives in Austin, Texas.